SELMA, LORD, SELMA

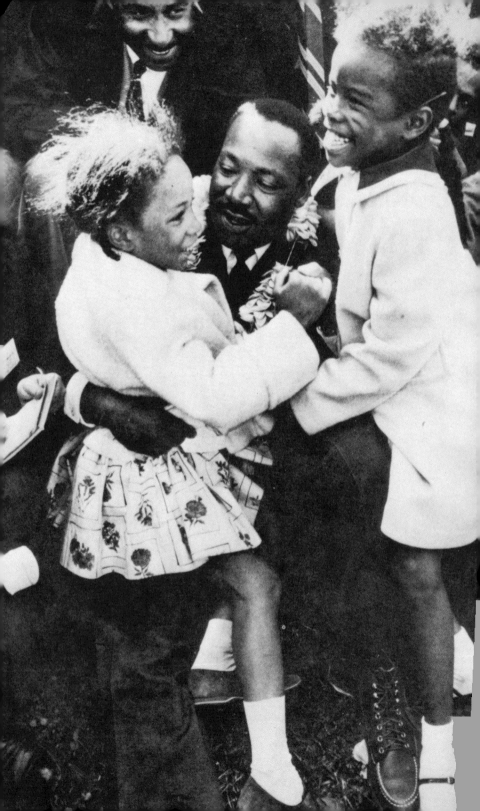

Sheyann Webb
Rachel West Nelson

SELMA, LORD, SELMA

GIRLHOOD MEMORIES OF THE
CIVIL-RIGHTS DAYS
as told to
Frank Sikora

THE UNIVERSITY OF ALABAMA PRESS
TUSCALOOSA AND LONDON

FRONTISPIECE: On March 21, 1965, Sheyann Webb, left, and Rachel West receive a victory hug from Dr. Martin Luther King, Jr., just before the start of the march from Selma to Montgomery. [© 1979 Vernon Merritt-Black Star]

Paperback Printing 1997

Library of Congress Cataloging in Publication Data

Webb, Sheyann.
    Selma, Lord, Selma.

    1. Webb, Sheyann. 2. Nelson, Rachel West.
3. Afro-Americans—Civil rights—Alabama—Selma.
4. Selma, Ala.—Race relations. 5. Afro-Americans—
Alabama—Selma—Biography. I. Nelson, Rachel West,
joint author. II. Sikora, Frank, 1936– III. Title.
F334.S4W3   301.45'19'6073022   [B]   79-19327
ISBN 0-8173-0898-9

3 4 5   01 00 99

To our parents and brothers and sisters,
and to the memory of Dr. King who said,
"Walk together, children, and don't ya grow weary."

CONTENTS

List of Illustrations   viii
Foreword   ix

SELMA, LORD, **SELMA**   1

Afterword   145

ILLUSTRATIONS

Martin Luther King, Jr., Sheyann Webb, and
Rachel West, March 21, 1965   *frontispiece*

Sheyann Webb, 1965   5

Rachel and Sheyann, 1965   9

Rachel West, 1965   13

Jonathan Daniels   52

Martin Luther King in Selma, February, 1965   65

Sheriff's deputies keep prospective black voters in line   65

Sheyann and Rachel at street meeting near church   78

"Bloody Sunday," March 7, 1965   89, 90, 91

Deputies hem in demonstrators in wake of Bloody Sunday   109

The Selma Wall   113

A prayer vigil near Brown Chapel   113

Ms. Sheyann Webb, at age 19, with Mrs. Coretta King   135

Ms. Sheyann Webb, 19, during tenth-anniversary observance
of Bloody Sunday   138

Mrs. Rachel West Nelson, 1979   141

Brown Chapel AME Church and Memorial, 1979—
"... a tribute to those who planned, encouraged, marched,
were jailed, beaten and died to change black Americans
from second class to first class citizens."   147

FOREWORD

On January 2, 1965, Reverend Martin Luther King, Jr., came to Selma, Alabama, to recruit an army of nonviolent soldiers to wage a war against laws and customs that prevented blacks from voting.

Being a black American living in Selma didn't mean you automatically became a part of this army. The decision to join up was a matter of individual conscience for each man, woman, and child. Many did not volunteer.

Those who did made the choice at different times and under varying circumstances. This is the story of two members of that army, two young girls: Sheyann Webb, who was eight, and her friend and next-door neighbor Rachel West, age nine.

Neither emerged from her experiences an Afroamerican Joan of Arc, but both of them saw the battle erupt, both saw it through, and both lived to see the conclusion.

It could be argued that both merely took part, that they merely followed their elders, that neither could be described as a heroine.

But it also could be argued, just as surely, that to characterize their actions as anything less than heroic would be to do them both an injustice.

It wasn't until March 1975—exactly ten years after the event in Selma known as "Bloody Sunday"—that I met Sheyann Webb. It was a short time after that that I met Rachel West Nelson. They had been young girls during the 1965 voting-rights drive. Now they were in their late teens. We decided, while their memories of the events in which they participated were still vivid, to tell as much as possible of their part in what happened.

This work is not an attempt to chronicle the civil-rights movement in Selma; most of what happened there is not even mentioned. It is not even a day-by-day report on the lives of two little girls who were part of the undertaking that made Selma an epic battleground in the Afroamerican petition to gain the rights promised by America's founders. What follows are simply the two girls' recollections, many years later, of an important time in their lives—a span of about three months, January through March 1965.

In today's journalism, oral history and tape recordings often go hand-in-hand. There were, however, no tapes used in preparing this work, and I doubt that what follows is oral history, at least in the strict sense of the term. The recollections set forth here are the product of newspaper-style interviews, about forty in all, conducted for the most part in the living rooms or kitchens of the family units in the George Washington Carver Homes from March 1975 through March 1979. Detailed, often verbatim notes were taken.

The recollections of the two young women did not

occur exactly in the order in which they are presented, and many of them came to light in response to questions (some of which were suggested to me by the interviewees' associates), rather than spontaneously. Thus, the chapters of this book did not develop in one sitting; each combines material gathered in two or more separate interviews with one or both women. After a number of interviews, I put the girls' thoughts into writing—editing, shaping, and condensing their recollections into continuity, and occasionally inserting bracketed material when necessary for clarity. The final results were carefully checked for accuracy by the girls themselves. Thus, the text as given here can properly be identified, and should be identified, as theirs, except for a number of passages of background information designed to put events into better focus; these passages, by the interviewer, are printed in different type so that the reader can easily distinguish between them and the interview material.

Throughout the interviewing process, I wasn't interested in learning all of what had happened in Selma in 1965 so much as I was in how the two girls had *felt* about what they had experienced. For instance, it wasn't enough to know simply that they had "feared death" in those times; I needed to know in what ways that fear was felt, and how they had dealt with their fears. In Sheyann's case, I learned, through questioning, that it meant writing her own obituary. For Rachel, it meant talking aloud to a statue of the Blessed Virgin Mary.

Why seek out the recollections of two children,

when there were so many intelligent, articulate adults in the Selma marches? Really, it was a picture that convinced me that such a story needed to be told—a picture of a little girl arrested during the Birmingham civil-rights demonstrations of 1963. Attired in a white dress, she stood forlorn, yet with a quiet pride as she waited to be taken to jail. That photo was just one of many in a thick file in the library of *The Birmingham News*. As I had leafed through the folder, it had literally jumped at me. Who *was* that child? Did anyone know her name? Would anyone *ever* know it?

It was shortly after this, while I was in Selma, that the Reverend Frederick Reese was talking to me about the 1965 marches and particularly of the day when state troopers and mounted possemen had turned back the first attempt by blacks to march from Selma to Montgomery. "They were hitting men, women, and children . . ."

"What children?" I interrupted. "Who were they?"

Without a second's hesitation, he replied: "Sheyann Webb and Rachel West."

I knew then that, although the little girl in the Birmingham photograph might never be identified, I would be able to identify at least some in the legions of anonymous children who had displayed such incredible courage not only in Selma but also in Birmingham, Montgomery, Tuskegee, and many other places in the South. Sheyann Webb and Rachel West are but two of many, many children.

There is no plot, per se, to this work, and if there is a

message to be discerned, it is simply that children, too, can be a powerful force in the efforts of a people to achieve.

Certainly, there was a measure of courage that Sheyann and Rachel had to draw upon, fearing, as each did, that awful consequences could befall them at any time. This is the essence of their stories. Surely, if there is something compelling about the dreams and efforts of a people to overcome, to achieve a full freedom, that struggle strikes an even more responsive chord when it is seen through the innocent eyes of children.

There are many who helped gather background material, and I am grateful to them. They include, in addition to the Reverend Mr. Reese, the Reverend L. L. Anderson and the Reverend Lorenzo Harrison; Mrs. Margaret Moore, who died in 1975 in a boating accident; Mrs. Marie Foster; Thelma Wilmer, Debbie Pettaway, Cheryl Curtis Strong, Jimmie Miller, and Ann Moss (who also helped type the manuscript); Mayor Joseph T. Smitherman; Carl Morgan, Jr., Stan Sikes, Randall Miller, Rose and Henry Sanders and J. L. Chestnut; former sheriff and public safety director Wilson Baker, who died in 1976; and Cecil Jackson, who died in 1978. All are or were from Selma.

A special note of thanks to U.S. Appelate Judge Frank M. Johnson, Jr., of Montgomery; Orzell Billingsley of Birmingham; Frank Lee of Tuskegee, Victor Hanson, Jim Jacobson and Clarke Stallworth of *The Birming-*

ham News; to Malcolm M. MacDonald, James Travis, and Francis Squibb of The University of Alabama Press; and particularly to my wife Millie.

Rachel West Nelson, in recalling those turbulent days in 1965, said it seemed to her that something "divine" was taking place, and that even today she can stand on the street by Brown Chapel AME Church and "hear" the sounds of the freedom songs that were so loved and so hated in those times in Alabama. I can attest personally to this feeling, which is much the same as what one feels who "hears" the muffled sounds of conflict at some Civil War battlefield.

Finally, a word about the title of this work.

Sheyann Webb remembered often singing a song called Come By Here, Lord. It was one of the freedom songs. At the conclusion of the number, Sheyann went on to say, she and the others in the rallies would be so moved and inspired that they would continue the singing, stretching the song with such utterances as "come by here, Lord, come by Selma, Lord, Selma . . ."

Birmingham, Alabama   FRANK SIKORA
July 1979

SELMA,
LORD,
SELMA

"The efforts of American Negroes to secure for themselves the full blessing of American life must be our cause, too. Because it is not just Negroes, but really it is all of us who must overcome the crippling legacy of bigotry and injustice.

"And we shall overcome.

"The cries of pain and the hymns and protests of oppressed people have summoned into convocation all the majesty of this great government."—President Lyndon Baines Johnson, addressing the nation on the pending voting-rights bill and the plight of black Americans in Selma, Alabama, March 15, 1965.

CHAPTER ONE

It began on the chilly morning of January 11, 1965, as a little girl left her family's apartment at 312E of the George Washington Carver Homes in Selma, Alabama, and started the two-block walk to school. She was slim, pretty, and bright-eyed, with a slightly upturned nose. Her hair was in pigtails and the ribbons tied about them fluttered as she bounced along. Sheyann Webb was eight, a third-grader at Clark School.

Sheyann

People ask me when I joined the movement in Selma. And I can't really answer, because it wasn't a formal thing. You didn't enlist. You just were, or you weren't.

My name is pronounced like the capital city of Wyoming, but most called me "Shey" for short. You drop the e so it sounds like *shy*. I was always smaller than the other kids and some didn't even think I was eight. I remember on that morning that I had walked down the sidewalk that runs through the middle of the project lawn. The apartments are made of red brick and they cover several blocks. They had been built in the fifties for black people (we were called Negroes at that time). As I got to the street that day, Sylvan Street, I stopped to look for cars and as I did I looked to my right and I saw these white ministers standing outside Brown Chapel AME Church. It surprised me to see

them there; so I stood there wondering what was
going on. I also saw some of the people who had
come with Dr. King, as well as some of the Negro
people from Selma. Dr. King wasn't there, but I knew
it had something to do with the movement, because I
had gone to the church on January the second and he
had talked about leading marches and seeking our
freedom. I knew something was going to happen.
People had been coming and going around the apartments for several days.

So I kept standing there, my books in my arms, just
staring at those people. Time began to get away from
me. I knew school would be starting soon, but I didn't
move. Finally, the people went inside the church. That
church was right at the backdoor of our apartment; it
had been built back around 1900, and was made of
red brick; it had two steeples on it. Well, when they
had all gone inside, I started to cross the street, headed
for school. A car went by and I waited.

Then, for reasons I can't explain, I just turned and
went down the sidewalk to the church. I knew it was
probably wrong. But it didn't feel wrong. Something
inside me just told me I belonged in there, that what
was going on inside there was more important than
school.

There were about forty or fifty people inside and I
sat in the back. Nobody paid me much attention, so I
just sat there, sucking my fingers (it was a habit I'd had
since I was little), listening to what was being said.

One of Dr. King's aides, Hosea Williams, talked

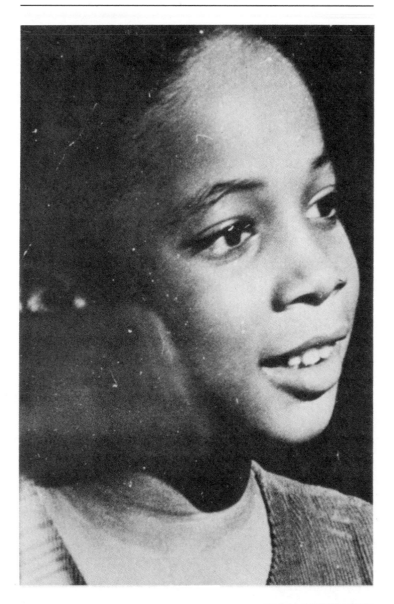

Sheyann Webb, 1965

about how only three hundred of the twenty-eight thousand Negroes in Selma and Dallas County were registered to vote—it was even worse in neighboring Wilcox and Lowndes counties, where none was allowed to vote.

" If you can't vote," he said, "then you're not free; and if you ain't free, children, then you're a slave."

I had to think about that as I sat there that day, because it was true. My own parents couldn't vote. They hadn't even tried to register, because they knew they didn't have a chance.

I remembered what Dr. King had said during the Emancipation Day program here on January the second:

"We are willing, and *must* be willing, to go to jail by the *thousands* in Alabama—"

He couldn't finish that pledge because he had been interrupted by a loud cheer and applause.

You had to *hear* Dr. King to really get his message. It wasn't just *what* he said, but *how* he said it. When he said that about be willing to go to jail by the thousands, the word "thousands" wasn't said, it was more like a quivery vibration in a loud and urgent stage whisper, and the part of the word, *thouuu,* just rolled through the church.

Without really thinking about it in so many terms, I just became, that day, a part of the movement to gain our freedom. Before there could be those thousands, there had to be one of us at a time.

I would stay at the church for five hours that day.

It was around one o'clock in the afternoon that the meeting ended for a lunch break. I went outside then; the sunshine was bright and it struck me that I better get to school. (I couldn't go home, because the door was locked.) With some reservations, I made the decision to go on. Mrs. Bright, my teacher, wouldn't take too kindly to me coming in this late. I remember I ran then, all of a sudden, just bolted across the street and ran between the apartments.

When I got to the school—it was a white frame building then, which always smelled of pencil shavings and chalk dust—I hesitated, then went in. It was a mistake.

The door creaked loudly when I turned the knob; all eyes were on me as I came in. There was a pause: Then: "Sheyann Webb! Where have you been, young lady?" Mrs. Bright is looking at me. She glances at her watch. "You know what time it is?"

I didn't know. I shook my head.

"It's twenty minutes past one. Where have you been?"

"Over there," I said.

"Over where? The church?"

"Yes, ma'am."

"You was over at Brown Chapel?" Louise Bright was upset with me. "Don't you know what kind of meeting they're having over there? That's a voting-rights meeting, child. That's not for children like you. Don't you know there might be trouble—might be folks put in jail. You want to be put in jail?"

I didn't know about that, so I just shrugged.

The lecture went on and I remember all the kids looking at me and I was so embarrassed. I bit my lip and flexed my leg muscles as hard as I could. But I started to cry.

And I think I made up my mind that day that I wasn't going to get in that situation again.

My momma was home from work when I got there that afternoon and I told her about missing school. Momma sewed shirts at Selma Apparel Company; my daddy worked at Cleveland Furniture Company. They had both worked hard. Even though Momma had eight children—one each year for eight years in a row—she was still slim and pretty.

So she wanted to know why I had missed five hours of school and why I had been at the church. And I told her about what had been said about us still being slaves.

I wanted to know if that was true.

She said we weren't, not like her great-grandmommas had been. But we were certainly second-class citizens, she said.

I wanted to know why. And she couldn't answer. So I told her I thought it was true, and that I was going to miss school again and go back to the church the next day. And I remember what she said to me: "If you want to grow up and be somebody, you gotta stay in school. Look at me. I'm thirty-four years old and the only job I can get is sewing shirts. You want something better for yourself."

Rachel, left, and Sheyann, 1965

Then she tells me that there's another reason for not missing school—the fact that going to the demonstrations can lead to serious injury, or something even worse.

"Like those little girls in Birmingham," she said, "that got killed at that church when somebody put a bomb in it. They wasn't doin' nothin' but bein' at church, and they got killed for it."

Momma tells me she don't want that to happen to me. I don't want it to happen, either, I tell her. "But if we don't do these things, like Dr. King say, then nothin' will ever change."

That night as I lay in bed, I thought about what was happening here in Selma. And to me. My older sister, Vivian, who was fifteen, had been in the demonstrations in 1964. Nothing had been won then. She had been arrested and put in jail. I didn't go to court, but my momma did and she had to beg the judge, B. A. Reynolds, to let Vivian come home. He had told her that Vivian "didn't know how to talk to a white man" and was going to put her back in the cell. But he finally let her go; she had been so upset that she went to New York to live with some relatives. If she had been here, I thought, she'd be at the church with me.

I had missed Vivian. I wished she could be here with the rest of us: Albert was seven, Joyce, ten, Dan, eleven, George, twelve, Sam, thirteen, and Johnny, fourteen. I knew Momma wanted what was best for all of us. She didn't want me to go to the church because she was afraid. She was afraid she and Daddy would lose their jobs. She was afraid I might be hurt.

So I lay there thinking about it. I was almost asleep when I saw the figure against the hall light and I heard Momma whisper hoarsely, "Don't forget, school tomorrow. Okay?"

I didn't answer. She kept staring at me; finally, concluding I must have been asleep, she eased away.

I knew that night that everything was going to be changing and I was going to be a part of it. Dr. King had said we would have to be a mighty army of nonviolent soldiers, men, women, and children, who would attack the hostility of the old plantation South at its most vulnerable point—through the conscience of the nation.

I kept thinking about the words Hosea Williams had said about if you can't vote, then you're a slave. So many black people not only could not vote, but they were even afraid to *try* to register. I knew that night that being a part of that nonviolent army Dr. King had spoken of was going to be the most important thing in my life.

I thought of the stanza in the song *We Shall Overcome* that "God is on our side." With the depth that only a child's mind could feel, I believed those words, believed them dearly.

CHAPTER TWO

A dank wind whistled through the apartment complex the next morning as Rachel West left for school. She was nine, a little taller than Sheyann; her eyes had an eternally mischievous glow

that dominated a pretty face framed by ribboned pigtails. She
lived at 313E, next door to the Webbs. Her parents, Mr. and Mrs.
Lonzy West, had eleven children. This was the beginning of the
storm season in Alabama, a time when occasional cold fronts
collided with masses of tepid, moist air blowing out of the Gulf of
Mexico, one hundred and fifty miles to the south of Selma.
Rachel knew the pattern: a couple of cold, clear days, a day or
two of warming temperatures, then the erratic, windy days as the
two fronts began to clash. The raucous skies would crackle with
thunder and explode torrents of rain. On those days, Sylvan
Street always resembled a small stream rushing dead leaves and
twigs over the curb.

Rachel

I was a Catholic and even though I went to St.
Elizabeth Mission School, I sometimes walked as far
as Clark School with Shey. If she didn't come by for
me, I'd go get her. So as I came out the door that day, I
looked and there she was standing down on the curb
of Sylvan Street. The street is about twenty-five yards
or so from our front door. I had called to her and she
waved.

"You ready to go?" I asked. I was in a hurry. My
school was about five blocks further.

She had shrugged. "I guess." But she kept standing,
looking at the church. "You know what they doin'
there, Rachel?"

"Sure. They plannin' to have a big march
downtown next Monday. They was talkin' about it last
night."

Shey looked at me. "Who was talkin'?"

Rachel West, 1965

"A bunch of people. They moved in with us and they gonna stay with us. They gonna take part in them marches. They say there's gonna be a big rally at the church Sunday night and Dr. King's comin' and they marchin' on Monday." We had crossed the street then; the wind was getting strong. I kept a hand on my bonnet to keep it from blowing. "Come on, Shey. We gonna be late."

As we walked, we spoke about the upcoming marches. There had been talk of people being arrested. Maybe even hurt. Or killed. Sheyann asked if that thought scared me. It did and I shuddered. "I don't want to be killed. Does it scare you?"

She shrugged. "Sure."

I had walked several more paces when I realized I was alone; turning, I saw she had stopped and was looking back toward the church. Hurry, I told her. I couldn't be late.

"You wanna go to the church with me?" she asked. "Come go with me, Rachel."

"We get in trouble if we miss school," I said. "Come on."

I left her standing there and learned later that she had missed. The church meetings being held that week were strategy sessions of the Southern Christian Leadership Conference. Dr. King's aides were meeting with local black leaders such as the Reverend F. D. Reese, Reverend L. L. Anderson, and others to plan the marches and demonstrations.

My mother, Alice West, had already told me what

might happen. She and my father were already committed to take part and we were among the first
families to take in those aides of Dr. King's who
needed a place to stay. We had stayed up late the
night before listening to them tell of other cities where
there had been demonstrations to integrate lunch
counters and get jobs for blacks. But Selma, they said,
would be even more important because we would be
trying to gain the right to vote. We might find trouble
because Sheriff Jim Clark had such an awful temper,
they said.

That day at school, one of the nuns told us that we
must remember to pray for peace in Selma, and ask
the Lord to guide us when the demonstrations began. I
remember asking if it would be all right for me to pray
at Brown Chapel even if it wasn't a Catholic church.

She had smiled at the question.

That afternoon it began to rain, a swirling, chilly
mist. I didn't hurry, though, just walked around the
puddles, head down, wondering about what lay
ahead. There had been talk the night before about
children in Birmingham being sprayed with hoses by
firemen. And about the bomb that killed four girls.

I found Sheyann at the church; she was standing
outside, under the protection of the front-door en-
trance. It was curious, but as I came up the steps, we
didn't say a word. The rain was falling harder and we
stood watching. If we had been total strangers, we
would have exchanged a greeting, spoken of the
weather. But here were two friends standing side-by-

side and remaining silent. I don't know what she was thinking about, but in my mind I was envisioning a march through that rain and wondering how many people might join it. And would it not anger Sheriff Clark even more if he had to be out in such a torrent because of us?

About fifteen or twenty minutes went by when we saw the sheriff's-department car going slowly along the street, stop for several moments in front of the church, then move on. I turned slightly to look at Sheyann. Her eyes met mine. "See that?" she asked.

"See what?" I said.

She squinted. "That car."

"What car?" Suddenly I burst out laughing.

"You!" she shouted.

I ran down the steps into the rain and she chased behind me. I cut left along the sidewalk between the church and the backdoors of the apartments. We laughed as we ran; our shoes squished.

As I look back on those days, it occurs that so much that was to happen in the months of January, February, and March, 1965, would take place in the rain.

CHAPTER THREE

"Martin [King] wanted to sort of ease into things and wait a little while before trying to integrate the Hotel Albert. But I told him, 'Why wait? Let's do it now. Nothing's going to be changed a week from now unless we start changing it.' So he agreed we'd

go on and do it, and this guy comes up and punches him."—
Reverend Fred Shuttlesworth, remembering January 18, 1965 in
Selma.

Sheyann

During those early days of the church meetings, before the first marches, I would be the only child there.
I'd sit in back and listen. I hadn't told my mother and
father about missing school.

It was on the third or fourth day that Theo Bailey,
who was about sixteen at the time, came back to where
I was sitting and asked me why I wasn't in school.

I thought for a moment, then asked him: "Why ain't
you?"

"I'm taking some time off," he said.

And I replied, "Me too."

Later, he had introduced me to Hosea Williams,
and after we had talked for awhile Williams had asked
me if I could sing. I told him I could. So we began
practicing singing some of the freedom songs—*Ain't
Gonna Let Nobody Turn Me 'Round, O Freedom, This
Little Light of Mine,* and some of the others. I knew
them all. So it was decided—and I don't remember
exactly how—that I would be singing at some of the
mass rallies to be held.

So I was now a part of the movement; the worry I
had had about missing school vanished.

That evening when Rachel got home, we walked
around the block several times, talking about the
meetings. I told her about the songs.

"You gonna sing up there in front of everybody?"
she asked. "Ain't you gonna be scared?"

"I don't know," I said. "I never been up there before a bunch of people."

There were more than eight hundred people at that
first rally held at Brown Chapel the night of Sunday,
January seventeenth, and some of the teachers were in
that crowd. I didn't look at them.

Rachel and I—dressed in our best dresses and wearing ribbons—sat in the front row; I think we must have
arrived an hour early. The Reverend Reese started the
meeting with a short talk about the first march to be
held the following day. After several minutes, he said
it was time for a song and called for me.

I sang and the people all joined in. After a few
stanzas of *Ain't Nobody Gonna Turn Me 'Round,* I
noticed that Rachel was up there with me, beaming
and singing her heart out. We would do a lot of singing together in the coming weeks.

Now, the singing at those meetings had a purpose;
it wasn't just for entertainment. Those songs carried a
message. They were different from Negro spirituals,
which—as beautiful as they are—told of some distant
hope while carrying the burdens of this life. Freedom
songs cried out for Justice right now, not later.

The words were simple and clear. They could be
changed to meet the needs of the time:

Ain't gonna let George Wallace turn me 'round,
turn me 'round, turn me 'round,

Ain't gonna let George Wallace turn me 'round,
  I'll keep a-walkin', I'll keep a-talkin',
Marchin' up to freedom lan'.

They spoke of our determination, our dignity:

We shall not, we shall not be moved,
  We shall not, we shall not be moved,
Just like a tree that's planted by the water,
  We shall not be moved.

And some told of the ultimate sacrifice we were prepared to make to achieve a dream:

O freedom, o freedom,
  O freedom's over me, over me,
And before I'll be a slave,
  I'll be buried in my grave,
And go home to my Lord
  And be free.

Monday, January 18, was sunny and cool in Selma. There was a whole crowd of people waiting outside the church when I left the house. Dr. King was to arrive sometime that morning and the first march was to be held. As I waited, squinting up the street for a glimpse of him—for some reason I thought he'd come walking down Sylvan Street—I listened as some men talked about Sheriff Clark having a group of deputies waiting at the courthouse.

"Man, they got their clubs," one of them said. It made me more than a little nervous. I couldn't know—and surely didn't know—that the mayor of

Selma, Joseph Smitherman, and the public safety director, Wilson Baker, had reached an "agreement" with the sheriff that there would be no undue force used. None of us could know that. So we waited with an air of uncertainty, but also with resolve and anticipation. Somebody started singing and the rest of us joined in; the singing bolstered our spirits.

Suddenly a woman shouted, "There he comes," and a long black car seemed to swish to the front of the church; there was a cheer as Dr. King alighted, smiling and waving. Because of my size, I couldn't get a good look at him. The crush of people straining forward wedged me to the fringes.

It wasn't long then that we began lining up on the sidewalk.

It occurred to me then that on this day, at any moment after the first step, somebody might die. We began moving forward, walking two or three abreast. It was about two blocks to Alabama Avenue and there Baker stopped us. I later learned that he told Dr. King that we didn't have a parade permit. So we broke up into small groups and walked piecemeal to the downtown.

Some of the people went into restaurants and stores with lunch counters and were served. I stayed with Mrs. Margaret Moore and we walked through the downtown for several minutes, then returned to the church. It wasn't until later that I learned that a white man attacked Dr. King as he registered at the Hotel Albert, located on Broad Street.

That night at the rally, me and Rachel sang again. There would be another march the next day, we were told. There was a tremendous cheer. Until then, I had been a little disappointed in the size of the crowd that had turned out for the march. But when I heard the shouting and the applause, I felt more confident.

I remember it was during one of those first rallies that I got up there by myself and sang a song that surely told what we had to face:

I went down to the County jail,
    Had no money to pay the bail,
Keep your eyes on the prize,
    O Lord, O Lord.

CHAPTER FOUR

"What is it they [the blacks] really want? Is it really the vote and good of our Negro citizens? Is it simply to sow discord and trouble?"—From a prepared statement of the Dallas County Board of Registrars, January 21, 1965.

Rachel

Coming home from the church that night of January 18, I more than anything, wanted to miss school and march that next day. I made up my mind that I would just stay out and go with Shey.

My mother was fixing cups of instant coffee in the

kitchen, and soon the visitors to our home—James Bevel and the others—came in. I would talk to her later, I thought.

There weren't enough chairs in the kitchen or the living room and people were sitting on the floor, drinking coffee and talking. The next day would be rough, they said. The word had come to us that Sheriff Clark would no longer abide by any "agreements" made earlier that day.

"We'll have some folks arrested tomorrow," my father had said. "That sheriff'll be after us."

He had been with the marchers that day and, he said, he had sized up the situation. There had been looks of hostility from many white bystanders. And Sheriff Clark, he added, had looked like a caged tiger, stalking about, fuming.

I don't think I can ever describe the feeling I had on that night and the others that followed. There was a togetherness, a camaraderie that would never again be felt in the years to come. I lay on the living room floor, listening to the grown-ups talk about the pending trouble that could, and would, come.

Folks were going to have to lay their bodies on the line, James Bevel was saying. He was one of Dr. King's aides. Nella, seventeen, who was my oldest sister, sat cross-legged on the floor, listening. The others of us were sprawled around beside her, wondering about what was ahead as we listened.

There was Juliette, thirteen, Diane, ten, Charlene, sixteen, Alice, fourteen, Roderick, eight, Mark, six,

and Carl, twelve. The littlest was Bonnie, age four. I'm
not sure she knew what was going on for sure, but she
sat up with us like she did. Lonzy, Jr., eighteen, was
living in Cincinnati at the time.

The people were saying that Dr. King can't do this
thing by himself; it's going to take people, people,
people. These white folks aren't going to back down
for nothing. It's going to take people out there every-
day. There's going to be people arrested, thrown in
jail, maybe even some gettin' their heads busted. It
may be even worse than that. We just didn't know.

The things that frightened me the most were the
horsemen Sheriff Clark had—they were called
"possemen"—and the thought of somebody planting
a bomb at the church; or a sniper.

I could imagine Brown Chapel erupting in smoke
and flame as had the Sixteenth Street Baptist Church in
Birmingham [on September 15, 1963] when Addie
Mae Collins, Cynthia Wesley, Denise McNair, and
Carole Robertson had died. I never knew them personally, but there was a kinship between all us black
folks, a bond that tied the Montgomery bus-boycott
people to the Birmingham people and finally to us
here in Selma.

Here, there was more at stake than just sitting at a
counter or having a "white only" sign removed from a
public restroom or riding in front of a bus. Gaining the
right to vote would, in itself, Bevel was saying, open
up all the other doors that had been closed.

We stayed up very late that night; the talk continued

and later somebody started singing softly—some of
the freedom songs—and the rest of us hummed along.
Then we prayed. The message was clear: We could
not be afraid—not of the bombs, nor the clubs, nor
those horses Jim Clark had, nodding and tossing in the
alley behind the courthouse. I had been told of them
that day.

My brothers and sisters, one by one, fell asleep on
the floor, and my father would pick them up and carry
them to their bedroom. But I fought the sleep. Outside,
the wind on this winter night made buzzing and whin-
ing sounds as it whipped through the apartments.

It had been such a special night. Here we were,
Catholics, Baptists, whites, blacks, all in one place;
we had all been to Brown Chapel and what denomi-
nation you were made no difference. That night convinced me that what was happening in Selma would
not just be Dr. King's movement, or the people's
movement, but something greater. Something, I
thought, almost divine. I fell asleep in the comfort that
I was being watched over.

In our house wanting to march and marching were
two different things. When I asked next morning if I
could miss school, my mother was very short. "Miss
school? And have the sisters coming here looking for
you? No, ma'am!"

It would be later in the movement before she would
change her mind.

CHAPTER FIVE

On January 19, 1965, Martin Luther King, Jr., led the second of a series of marches and demonstrations in Selma, in protest against Alabama's strict voting tests, which were designed—particularly in the Black Belt counties of the state—to prevent Negroes from registering. These counties were originally named the Black Belt because of their rich limestone soil, which had, through the centuries, become a dark loam. The name had taken on an ethnological meaning, however, because the majority of the people living in the area were the dark-skinned descendants of slaves. This had been plantation country, and in 1965 many features of the old order of antebellum life still flourished. It was a region of contrasts—majestic homes and ramshackle shanties, set against the endless sweep of cottonfields. Dallas County, of which Selma was the seat, was in the center.

Sheyann

I was the youngest, certainly the smallest, of the "regulars" in the demonstrations. And I was the first of the children. The others would start in February. But when I went I was the only one missing school. This march was on another sunny, but cold, day. We gathered at Brown Chapel that morning and sang songs and listened to the leaders—among them Dr. King and Hosea Williams—telling us why we were there and how to march, like two abreast. I was with Mrs. Margaret Moore again.

We started up the sidewalk. I think there must have been two hundred and fifty of us, I'm not sure. It wasn't a great number, I know that.

Now, we knew that sooner or later we would have an encounter with Sheriff Jim Clark; it was going to happen on this day. I was about half-way or more back in the line of marchers, and as we went along we began singing some of the freedom songs. We went south to Alabama Avenue, then turned west; the courthouse was four blocks further. We passed the Selma City Hall, where a group of white people stood watching us. Some of them laughed, I remember, but I didn't hear any shouts or jeering. Then we got to the courthouse.

We had been there for twenty or thirty minutes, standing, talking, singing a few songs, when I heard this disturbance toward the front. Then folks began shouting and crying out; I saw the sheriff with a hand behind the neck of Mrs. Amelia Boynton, running with her and hollering. Before this had happened, Clark and Dr. King had exchanged some words. I didn't hear them. Then the incident with Mrs. Boynton took place. Later I learned that she had asked him if she could go into the courthouse, and he said she could, but added, "You stay inside once you get there." Well, it was the lunch hour and all the courthouse workers left so Mrs. Boynton came out and when the sheriff saw her, he just got mad. He ran her down the street to a sheriff's car and had her arrested and taken away to the city jail. It had happened so quickly that I didn't get scared, but all the people around me began to get excited.

Then the sheriff began to shout at us. Suddenly

people were moving, jamming together in a tight circle, edging together protectively, like a wagon train.

Deputies, with sticks and those long cattle prods moved toward us. I squeezed tight on Mrs. Moore's hand; there was a sudden urge to back away, even turn and run. Somebody shouted, "Y'all are under arrest!"

I looked up at Mrs. Moore. "Me, too? Are they arrestin' me?"

Her face was blank. "Don't be scared," she said. "Don't be. Just stay close. Don't let go of my hand."

I saw some of them deputies push our people, saw some of them use the cattle prods and saw men and women jump when the electric ends touched against their bodies. People were shouting. A man stumbled; a sign fell from my view as a marcher reacted to the shock. My toes were stepped on and I lost my balance several times as we were wedged together. Then they moved us away from the courthouse and began marching us down Alabama Avenue, back toward the city hall.

I was now holding onto Mrs. Moore with both of my hands, watching so I wouldn't get touched with one of the prods. We were being moved like cattle. But once we got away from the courthouse the shouting stopped and the deputies stayed about five yards away from the edges of the rank. A lot of people, black and white, were on the sidewalks, watching. We were taken to the city hall; the jail was located up on the second floor. We must have been there standing in line for about a half hour when an officer came to me and asked why I was there.

"Because they made us all come here," I said.

"I know that," he said. "But why are you here in the first place? Why aren't you in school, where you belong?"

I shrugged. I was a little afraid then.

"Who told you to go to the courthouse with these people?"

"Nobody. I just come."

"If nobody told you, then why did you come?"

"To be free," I said. Several of the people nearby muttered "Um-hmmns."

And he said, "If you want to be free, then go home. That's where you're free, not here. Go on home, now."

There were sixty people jailed that day, and while I wasn't one of them, I had come close. It taught me a lesson. I knew that being part of this movement would not be without its moments of fear. I had felt that fear that day; all the people had. But we had stayed together and by doing so had overcome it. At the time, I couldn't appreciate the historic significance of the day, that a pattern of passive resistance to the sheriff's anger and aggressive behavior was established. It would go on and reach a point where the sheriff would run out of jail space to put the people. The last thing I remembered that day as I left the city hall and walked home, was the sound of those people inside—some of them were singing.

Woke up this mornin'
With my mind stayed on freedom.

If they could sing, I thought, then I could go on marching.

It was later that day that my parents learned for certain—although I suspected my mother knew earlier—that I had been missing school. One of the teachers had called. My father, John Webb, was a stocky man of medium stature, and he had a temper. When he confronted me that evening with the truancy report, I looked for it to surface. At first, I didn't answer when he asked me why I had been missing.

"Now, John," said my momma, coming to my rescue, "Shey's goin' to the church and all because she believes it's right and because we can't vote."

"She's supposed to be in school." He was sitting on the couch in the living room. Then, to me, he said, "You wanna grow up to be dumb?"

I shook my head and told him, "But it don't do no good to be smart if you still be a slave."

"Who told you that?" he asked. "We're not slaves."

"But we ain't free, either. That's why we gotta march."

"Workin' folks don't have time to march," he said.

"Well, Daddy," I said, "don't you wanna be free?"

He had shaken his head, ending the discussion. Later, when I told him I wanted to continue in the demonstrations, he hadn't committed himself, but his eyes had twinkled a trace of amusement. I read the look as approval.

CHAPTER SIX

"If an American, because his skin is dark, cannot . . . vote for the public officials who represent him, if, in short, he cannot enjoy the full and free life which all of us want, then who among us would be content to have the color of his skin changed and stand in his place? Who among us would then be content with the counsels of patience and delay?"—President John Kennedy, June 11, 1963.

Rachel

It was during the early days of the movement that I first got to talk to Dr. King. It was after one of the church rallies at Brown Chapel. Shey and I had been sitting right up front and had sang some of the freedom songs.

After the rally, as Dr. King was going out the side door and while the other people were still singing, we had gotten up and ran to the back of the church and hurried outside and around to the door by the parsonage. He was already coming out, and when we ran up he stopped to speak to us.

I remember he said something about our singing, shook hands with us and then asked our names. Then he leaned down closer and said to us, "What do you want?"

And we said, "Freedom."

"What's that?" he says. "I couldn't hear you."

So we say, louder this time, "Freedom."

And he shakes his head and kind of smiles a little. "I still don't believe I heard what you said."

So we laugh, and then real loud we yelled, "We want freedom!"

"I heard you that time," he says. "You want freedom? Well, so do I."

We got to be friends from then on. Everytime he'd see us he'd play that little game with us, asking what we wanted, pretending he couldn't hear what we'd say until we were shouting at the top of our lungs, "Freedom!"

Sometimes, during the rallies at Brown Chapel, when Shey and I would sing, he would call us over where he would be sitting at the altar and lift us up on his lap and we'd sit there with him until it was time for him to speak. I'm sure many of the other people envied us. We'd be sitting up there so proud!

During the rallies, Shey and I were always at the church early and often we'd be back of the altar listening to Dr. King and the other leaders discussing strategy.

One night, and it must have been in that first week or so, Dr. King left one of those meetings and came to where we were and we talked. He told us about his family and said he had a girl about our age. Then he asked, "Do you young ladies have your marching shoes on?"

Well, we didn't know it was a figure of speech and both of us dropped our heads and examined our feet. And I remember I lifted up one foot so he could see better and very seriously said, "This is the only good pair I got."

So he nodded quietly. Then he said, "They'll do. They're just fine."

They were all I had; in fact, we didn't have much of anything in those days. Food was always short and sometimes we were hungry.

The coat I had—it was a padded one with a parka—was too short on me. So were my pants, which were hand-me-downs from my sisters; they reached well above the tops of my white socks.

My mother and father had a rough time keeping up with the bills and feeding all of us children. That's the truth. If the car broke down or somebody got sick it was a financial crisis, and the first place you noticed it was on the supper table. Our regular diet was rice and coffee—usually without milk—or greens and corn-bread. And coffee. I was practically raised on coffee.

I remember one evening waiting out in front of the church and hoping I'd get to see Dr. King. Well, he didn't come to the rally that night, but some civil-rights workers showed up with cardboard boxes full of lunch-meat sandwiches and cartons of milk and orange drink. There were a lot of kids out there and we converged on the workers, who began passing the food out to us. I remember jumping up and down with the other kids, trying to get to the front of the line, worrying that the supply would run out before I got up there. But I made it; the milk was gone, but there were cartons of orange Jungle Juice. The civil-rights movement had a practical purpose as well as the more lofty goal of achieving voting rights: It helped get us some food. An army marches on its stomach. Our nonviolent army in Selma traveled on bologna sandwiches and orangeade or milk.

CHAPTER SEVEN

On January 20, 1965, Lyndon Johnson was inaugurated to a full four-year term as president of the United States. He had spoken of complete freedom for all Americans, especially the right to vote. In Selma, registering to vote wasn't the immediate issue for blacks; the problem was just getting inside the Dallas County Courthouse.

Selma continued to bustle with civil-rights activity, but the pace wasn't as sharp as the Southern Christian Leadership Conference had hoped for. Then, on Friday, January 22, a march took place that spurred the imagination of the black community. F. D. Reese led one hundred and twenty-five black teachers from Brown Chapel to the courthouse, where he and they were prodded and pushed by the club-toting sheriff—while the television cameras of NBC captured it all for the nation. The teachers had been holding back, watching with apprehension and misgivings.

In those days, school teachers were the upper class among blacks in the South, the only professionals of their race in Black Belt counties. This march inspired other teachers to join the ranks and opened the way for teachers to allow their students to take part. An army of children was poised to join the effort.

Sheyann

I had heard that morning that the teachers might try the march but didn't know for sure until that afternoon (the twenty-second) when they began arriving at the church. I saw that some of them were holding up their toothbrushes, showing that they were prepared to go to jail. I remember standing outside there and listening to the Reverend Reese talk to them about how important they were, how important this march would be.

"The sheriff will think twice about mistreating you," he had said. "You are teachers in the public-school system of the State of Alabama, but you can't vote. We're going to see about that today. If they put us in jail, there won't be anybody to teach the children and he [Clark] knows if they're not in school, then they'll be out in the streets. And he doesn't want that."

They had sung several songs; then, with Reese in front, they began walking along Sylvan Street; I watched them move along the sidewalk, under the bare branches of the oak trees.

Rachel had arrived home and after hurriedly depositing her books inside, had come back; we ran up the street, watching as the teachers swung down Alabama Avenue toward the courthouse. We stopped at the corner, peering after them. Then, whooping with excitement, we had sprinted back to the church. By then other children had gathered; the word was spreading like electric: "The teachers are marching! The teachers are marching!"

Most of us had viewed the educators as stodgy old people, classic examples of true "Uncle Toms." But that wasn't the opinion that day. I looked about me and saw scores of other children running about the apartment complex shouting the news that Mr. Somebody or Old Mrs. Somebody was marching. Could you believe it? And, yes, I had seen Mrs. Bright there, too.

I had been to school only once since that first day I came in late; my momma had insisted that I walk Albert to his class the day before, which was Thursday. Albert had locked himself in the bathroom and didn't want to go because I wasn't going. Momma had been upset and, I believed, blamed me for his actions. She was late for work and told me to take him.

I had agreed and had to promise Albert that I'd take him with me on a march if he'd come out of the bathroom. Arriving at school, Mrs. Bright and several other teachers—who had been in the hallway talking—saw me. When she called my name, I froze. Well, I figured I was in bad trouble then; no need to be polite and say, "Yes, ma'am, Mrs. Bright?" I just stood there.

But she and the others had been very kind, not saying a word about my absences. Instead, she questioned me about the marches and what was being planned for the future, as far as the demonstrations were concerned. We talked for about ten minutes. I had edged toward the door then, and Mrs. Bright said, "Now you be careful out there, child. And come back to your class as soon as you can."

I told her I would.

On that 22nd of January, Reese had led the teachers to the courthouse and Clark had used his nightstick to push the marchers back from the door. School superintendent Joseph Pickard and members of the board of education stood by, urging the marchers to return to the church, and asking the sheriff to keep his patience. One board member said the teachers were setting a bad example for their pupils. For more than fifteen minutes the teachers had stood there waiting to be arrested, while Clark uttered warnings and made threatening gestures with his club. Finally, when it was apparent there would be no arrests, the teachers, jubilant at the courage they had found within themselves, returned to the church.

Sheyann

Some little boys came running down the street yelling that they were coming back. Me and Rachel went into the church which was packed with people. My momma and Rachel's momma had come over, too, sitting in the front. We waited and when the teachers began coming in everybody in there just stood up and applauded. Then somebody started to sing—I think it was *This Little Light of Mine.* Boy, did they sing! First one song and then another, as they walked in. And they were all smiling; kids were shaking hands with their teachers and hugging them. I had never seen anything like that before; I doubt that a scene like that will ever happen again. Some of the women teachers were crying, they were so elated. Mrs. Bright spotted me, and rushed forward, hugging me. She appeared to be in a mood of triumph. She laughed, she wiped at her eyes, she hugged me again.

I remember she said something about her feet being tired, and I said, "You did real good."

As I look back on that afternoon, it's clear that the reception given the returning teachers touched them, inspired them to take part in this drive for voting rights, for freedom. At the same time, they—with their dignity that astounded the white community—inspired many of the children as well as other adults. It was the interaction of people that would hold the movement together through the hard days ahead.

We would need that togetherness to sustain us because, after one week, nothing had changed, outwardly. More than two hundred of our people had been arrested, yet not one black had even gotten inside the courthouse to try to register to vote. And, in my case, my own parents had not yet taken active part.

I'd heard that some of the deputies had laughed about our efforts and had bragged that the score was "Jim Clark 250, Martin Luther Coon, zero."

CHAPTER EIGHT

A U.S. district judge, Daniel Thomas in Mobile, issued an order specifying that Sheriff Clark had to allow one hundred blacks a day in the registration line. When one hundred and twenty-three persons showed up, the extra twenty-three were counted off and arrested. It was raining but, as the sheriff pointed out, the court order hadn't said anything about waiting *inside.* So he allowed only one person inside at a time. All the others had to stand outside in the rain, waiting their turn to try to pass the registration test.

Rachel

Sometimes I wouldn't go straight home from school, but would head for the courthouse. My mother had told me I couldn't miss school to march; she'd never said anything about joining the demonstrators after classes.

I had trotted the last few blocks because I could see the crowd gathered at the front of the courthouse. Sheriff Clark was out there facing them and he was reading something. I learned later it was a court order by Judge William Hare, a circuit judge, forbidding assemblies and demonstrations within a certain distance of the building. The people were standing there listening and I heard the sheriff say something to the effect, "You must disperse from the area of the courthouse. This is an unlawful assembly. You're ordered to cease this gathering and disperse."

When he finished, he had held the paper down at

his side, then placed his hands on his hips, sort of like those pictures you see of General George C. Patton. There wasn't a sound for a few seconds, just the wind blowing. Then, from down at the far end, somebody started singing and it caught on all along the ranks.

We shall not, we shall not be moved,

"Shut up!" shouted the sheriff, and his voice was surprised and angry. "Stop that, now! You niggers cut that out!"

We shall not, we shall not be moved,

"I said stop it! Y'all stop that right now!" Clark was pacing about, he was so mad. "I said cut it out!"

Just like a tree that's planted by the water,
We shall not be moved.

I was on the right side of the marchers, on the outside of the ranks, holding hands with an elderly woman and a teenage girl; we did that when we sang, to show our unity. But even holding hands, I had a feeling in my stomach, a chill that made me shudder. I didn't want to be hit. I knew the horsemen were not far away, either. And the sheriff seemed to be getting awfully angry as we sang. Finally, his pacing stopped and raised a hand. "If you don't stop," he says, "if you don't stop right now, I'm going to arrest every one of you."

Well, the singing stopped; there was some movement in the ranks; the woman next to me, stepped away, moving closer to the main group in the center. It left me and the teenager off to ourselves, a few yards away from the main group. The sheriff was waiting for a response, waiting for us to leave. But from the center front, the singing started again. Nobody had signalled it, it just happened, a spontaneous thing.

"All right," said the sheriff. "Arrest 'em. Move 'em this way. Move 'em this way down the street."

There must have been two hundred and fifty people there, but the ranks weren't solid; the deputies didn't get all of them, only those who were close together near the center; the rest of us stood by, watching as about one hundred were taken away to jail.

I remember I hurried home then to tell what I had seen. It had been distressing to see the people arrested, to hear the sheriff rant at us. It hardly seemed like we were winning.

It was later that day—the sun was almost down behind the apartments—that things became even more troubled for me. I was playing down the street a way when I noticed the black car parked beside the church. It was the one Dr. King rode in. I went up there but he was inside the church. That's when I noticed the luggage inside the car. There were several people standing nearby and I asked them where he was and they told me he was going to Atlanta.

Atlanta, I thought. How could he go to Atlanta when we needed him here? I ran to Sheyann's house to tell her. She was lying in front of the television set, watching a cartoon with Albert and Joyce.

"Hey, Shey, Dr. King's goin' 'way!" I tell her.

She jumps to her feet. "Goin' 'way? When?"

"Right now," I say. I don't think she believed it. But she threw on her coat and we rush out the back door and down the back walkway, dodging the branches that hung over from the church property. Dr. King was already coming out of the parsonage, his briefcase in his hand. When she saw it, Sheyann believed. It crushed her as much as it did me.

When he saw us he waved.

"You leavin'!?" Sheyann says.

He told us he was going home for a little while but he would be back. We didn't like it, and he saw the disappointment. Then he told us that his children wanted to see him and he wanted to see them. Well, we could understand that, but we insisted that he tell us when he was coming back.

And he said, "I'll be back by Monday. Just keep your marching shoes on, because I'll be calling on you."

"We need you to march with us," I told him.

"You two watch over things until I get back," he said.

Still crestfallen, we nodded. If he wasn't here, I thought, who would be our leader? Who would lead the rallies?

We watched him duck into the car, heard the door slam. Sheyann stood there gazing at him, but I turned away. I didn't want to see him leave, even for a few days. Instead, I looked at the church.

The car motor started up, but there wasn't any movement. I heard the door open and I spun around. He had gotten out. To our surprise he hurried to us, leaned over and kissed me, then Sheyann, just a quick brush on the cheek.

"I love both of you," he said. Then he was gone. As the car pulled away, we waved and called to him that we would miss him. I don't know if he heard us or not, but he waved.

We stood there for a long time, even though we couldn't see the car anymore, staring up the street, not saying anything. I think I was hoping he'd somehow turn and come back to us.

We loved him, too.

CHAPTER NINE

"We kept hoping that the civil-rights stuff would bog down before there was any trouble. But [Sheriff] Clark just seemed to get suckered into these situations and make things worse. One day this black woman hauled off and belted him; she decked him. That got things stirred up. So I was trying to get this new industry to Selma, Hammermill Paper, and I was wining and dining them at the Plantation Inn and I get a call from Governor Wallace asking if I need troopers. I didn't want them, didn't think we needed them, but he sent them anyway. It was really getting edgy then. You see, the federal people were really concerned with Selma. We worried them. I was told that there was a plan to send paratroopers in here when there had been demonstrations in 1964. I mean it was an invasion plan: They weren't coming in on trucks, they were going to be *dropped* from planes. This whole civil-rights thing was like a war, like we were being invaded. It just kept growing and growing and we couldn't do anything about it."—Selma Mayor Joseph T. Smitherman.

Sheyann

My name was really Krisandra Sheyann, but everybody called me by the middle name, which I preferred. I don't know where Krisandra came from, other than the fact that my momma had liked it. Sheyann was a name that was handed down from her side of the family; my Great-Great Granmomma Wade had been named Sheyann. She had been a slave. Although we had never been able to find the exact site, the plantation where she had worked was located not far from Selma.

During those early days of the voting-rights drive in Selma, I found myself sometime thinking about Granmomma Wade. The stories she had told were limited because, Momma had told me, the people who had been slaves wanted to forget as much as they could.

One night, during that second week of the movement, I began to run a fever; I was coughing, my throat was getting raw.

"You been out in the cold and rain too much, young lady," Momma had said. Giving me orange-flavored baby aspirins and water, she insisted I stay in and go to bed. "Other folks can sing tonight."

I didn't argue with her, but lay listening to the wind blowing. It was good to be in a warm bed. I had been told that Granmomma Wade and the other slaves often lived in shanties with only one little stove for cooking and heat. Some of them had little clothing; I'd heard stories where they were even nearly naked when they worked in the field. I wondered if Sheyann Wade were living if she would be at the church. I bet she would. I bet she would have been in the marches.

Momma brought me some soup later, and we talked about Granmomma Wade.

"When they was freed," Momma said, "they all stayed right here in this county; I guess they didn't have no money to go up North. They just stayed right here and worked. And they didn't get paid much at all in them days."

I asked, "Did she say they ever tried to vote?"

Momma shrugged. "Well, in them days no women could vote, not even white ones. But she did say that some of the men did vote some but later they couldn't. The white folks had turned things around and cut them off. She said some tried later but the white men would tell 'em, 'Y'all niggers ain't ready to vote yet.' They put 'em off, and before long black folks just lose their rights."

I couldn't understand how that could happen.

"'Cause they was scared," Momma said. "Granmomma Wade used to talk a little about it. She said she'd seen folks whipped. Even though they got free, some of 'em didn't forget. And they wasn't educated."

"Did they ever beat Granmomma Wade?"

Momma shook her head. "She never did say. See, she was real old when I was a girl. She just never said a whole lot about it."

"You said them people who be slaves was scared," I had said. "So they never could vote. So today folks are still scared to go out there and they can't vote, either. See? We just like we was a whole hundred years ago."

She didn't answer me, just sat on the bed thinking, her eyes on the floor.

Later, almost asleep, I heard the sounds of the singing from the church; it seemed far away, almost a part of the wind. I lay there listening to the words:

O freedom, O freedom's over me,
  And before I'll be a slave,
I'll be buried in my grave,
  And go home to my Lord
And be free

All of a sudden the thought struck me: *I might die.*

I might be in a march and someone would shoot and I'd be hit. Or I might be in the church when a bomb went off. Or I might be singing in front of the courthouse and a deputy might hit me with a club. *I might die.*

I had envisioned what it might be like: I saw my momma and daddy crying, following a little white casket across a brown field. Rachel would be there, holding a prayer book and flowers. And who else would be there? Would anyone in this whole world

know? Or even care? I was very frightened. I jumped
out of the bed, snapped on the lamp and sat there for
more than an hour contemplating; I prayed for courage to face whatever was ahead. But it didn't halt the
quivering of my hand, the shaking in my legs.
Maybe it was the fever that made me think those
thoughts. But I took a piece of paper from the drawer,
found a pencil, and began printing:

SHEYANN WEBB, 8 YEARS, WAS KILLED TODAY IN SELMA.
SHE WAS ONE OF DR. KING FREEDOM FIGHTERS. SHE WAS A
STUDENT AT CLARK SCHOOL SELMA. SHEYANN WANT ALL
PEOPLE TO BE FREE AND HAPPY.

That done, I sat listening to the wind; it had such a
menacing groan. I looked about the room, then ran to
the door and hurried down the steps.
My momma and daddy slept in the bedroom
downstairs; I ran in and began tugging at Momma's
arm. She awoke, stared at me for a moment, then
asked, "What's the matter?"
I told her, "I be scared."
Then I crawled in beside her. She raised up on one
arm. "You been cryin'?" she asked.
"I scared I might die, Momma."
"What?" She was fully awake now. "Die! What you
talkin' 'bout?"
I told her about the thoughts, and she cradled me
close. "You not gonna die, doll," she crooned. "No,
ma'am, you ain't. You quit that bein' scared now and
go to sleep. You just lettin' all these things pile up and
weigh that little heart down, that's what happen. My

Lord, die! You ain't gonna die. I ain't lettin' nobody hurt my little girl."

She kept holding me close to her while I told her about the wind, how it had frightened me. Later, I fell asleep. But after that night my momma began taking part in the marches. She didn't join them, but everytime we marched, she'd walk beside us, and when we'd be at the courthouse, I'd see her standing over on the sidewalk, keeping her eyes on me.

In later years, Momma would say that it was my courage and persistence that made her actively join the movement in Selma. I don't know about that. But my fears surely played a part.

That cold or touch of flu that I had kept me sidelined for several days.

Sooner or later it affected a lot of people, even Dr. King, I think. I remember one night I went to the church and found him sitting alone in the study. He must have been tired, or maybe not feeling well, or worried. Anyway, when I walked in, he didn't look at me, just kept sitting there. Then, he heard me and turned; he didn't smile.

"What do you want?" His voice was sharp, like he was busy and didn't want to be bothered. It surprised me, and I just stood there.

Turning back to the papers he had been reading, he repeated: "What do you want?"

"Freedom," I said.

He had turned quickly then, facing me. "What?" Then his face softened and he smiled. "I'm sorry," he said. "That's what we all want."

CHAPTER TEN

The waning days of January erupted into a fury of wintry weather; the mercury, early of Saturday, January 30, dipped into the mid twenties, and when a march began that morning, flecks of snow were spat across the dun-colored flatlands of the Black Belt. In the absence of Martin Luther King, Jr., James Bevel led the march, followed by about a hundred people. It was a silent, stumbling walk. Puffs of frost billowed from the marchers' nostrils. A harsh wind whistled through Selma, numbing toes, stinging ears and noses, making their eyes glazed, limpid. The marchers sniffled and sneezed.

Rachel

I wore two pair of socks that day and had the hood of my coat tied as tightly as I could stand it. I wore pants. I couldn't have picked a worse day to join a march. It would have been easier to stay inside, sprawled on my belly watching the cartoons. But Shey and I had decided the night before that we'd put on our "marching shoes" and follow along.

When we arrived at the courthouse, we saw a deputy standing in the doorway drinking a cup of coffee. It looked so good. But then he went back in and we were left standing there. The wind was terrible; it went right through my coat, right in around my ears and down my back. Shey was even colder; she was wearing a dress and her legs were vibrating. My jaw was trembling so I could hardly talk.

After standing there for several minutes, Bevel led us singing *We Shall Not Be Moved*, but the words seemed to freeze. The cold took something out of our voices. But finally Sheriff Clark comes out of the court-house and tells us that the board of registrars is closed and for us to go home and quit blocking the sidewalk.

I couldn't imagine us blocking anybody from using the sidewalk, because there wasn't anybody out. They were inside where it was warm.

Clark's deputies were behind him, their hands in their pockets, their clubs and cattle prods sticking out from under their arms.

He repeated his order for us to leave. Well, James Bevel said that the people had come to register, that Negroes had been waiting a hundred years; and Sheriff Clark said something about we could wait another few days. I think he would have been happy to let us stand there and freeze, but we started singing again and the sheriff pointed his nightstick at Bevel and told his men to arrest him.

They took about twenty-five others and marched them off, while the rest of us danced back and forth from one foot to the other, singing, trying to get warm. There wasn't any sign of the sun; just gloomy grey clouds.

The wind was making us miserable and finally, in twos and threes, we moved back to Brown Chapel.

But I didn't go into the church. I ran to the apart-ment and went straight to the sink to run warm water over my hands.

That night there were more than eight hundred people at the church and what James Bevel said was true: That even though a federal judge [Thomas] had issued some kind of injunction against the sheriff to allow one hundred people to line up when the registrar's office was open, it wasn't that big of a deal, because we black folks had been living under an injunction for as long as we had been in America. We had been born under an injunction.

We had been enjoined from everything that white Americans took for granted.

We sang a song that night that had its origins as a spiritual, but the civil-rights movement had adopted it, sang it with a more rapid tempo. The simple words, I think, really captured the feeling that was in me and—I hoped—the others who were there.

> *This little light of mine*
>   *I'm gonna let it shine*
> *Everywhere I go,*
>   *I'm gonna let it shine,*
> *All through the night,*
>   *I'm gonna let it shine.*

White folks probably never understood how important our songs were to us, how they played such a role in binding us, bringing out what courage we had when things looked bleak.

That night, after singing that song through several times, I was ready to march again, no matter how cold it was outside, no matter how cutting the wind might be.

There was truly a deeper meaning to the songs we would sing, a religious one. That "little light" in each of us, I believed, was that spiritual strength and determination we instilled in ourselves that the Lord Almighty was walking with us, that we were never alone, that we were right.

It was as though each one of us was a candle or a star. By ourselves we were each nameless little souls unknown to the rest of the universe. But together we could be a glow that would light up Selma for the whole world to see.

Of all the people who came to stay with us during the movement my favorite was Jonathan Daniels, a seminary student from Keene, New Hampshire. He was a young person, young at heart, I mean. He was twenty-six and I think of him almost as a boy. He came to us in early February.

He was never a stranger, not Jonathan. From that first day he walked in with his suitcase and little knapsack, it was like an old friend coming home.

We children loved him. He would smile at the way we talked, and we'd laugh at his speech.

Jonathan would die for us.

But I had no way of knowing that then. I only knew that we liked being with him. He was always out playing with us. He'd take me and Shey on his knee and tell us stories, or he'd take us to the store and buy us candy or soft drinks. He often bought food for us.

He couldn't sit down in our house without me and Shey jumping up in his lap.

He had a way with him that drew children to him.

Jonathan Daniels, 26, of Keene, N.H., an Episcopal seminarian, was a special friend of both Sheyann (shown here) and Rachel, and "a member of every black family in Selma" in the civil-rights days.

Often, during the coming demonstrations, we would be near to him; he would hold our hands when we'd be in the street singing. He made me feel more secure when he was with me.

When Jonathan came to us, I knew for certain that there were really good white folks in this country, and with them on our side we would win our freedom.

One of the first ministers to come live with us was a Presbyterian priest named Samuel Morris. Now he had just planned to stay a few days but when he saw what was happening—this was in February, the early part—he decided he was going to stay; he sent for his wife and three children. One of them was a boy who was about seven and he was enrolled with us at St. Elizabeth Catholic School. So he would walk with us each day to and from classes. I think they put him there because it would have been too much trouble to enroll him in the public school; besides, he would be with us.

When we walked to school we'd often see some white kids who would be going to Parrish High School, which did not allow blacks to attend. They never bothered us. But this one day I saw some of them watching us as we walked with this little white boy. I remember there were some shouts at us, some hooting. But we kept walking. Next day, it was the same thing. Me and my sister Diane and this boy just kept walking; I was afraid to look at them or say anything. They were bigger kids, maybe fourteen or fifteen, maybe even older, some of them. Well, we got to school, but all that day I was worried about it, because it was the second day in a row they had been watching us. I guess it made them mad seeing us blacks walking to school with the white boy. I remember wishing it would rain hard so his father would come pick us up in his car. But it didn't happen. When we got out that afternoon me and Diane and the boy started home and we walked as fast as we could. The school was on Broad Street near Good Samaritan Hospital and we had to go across the railroad tracks, then to Jeff Davis, then turn left there and go another four blocks or so before we got to Sylvan Street. We'd be pretty safe there, because that's where the apartments started.

But before we got to the railroad tracks which crossed Broad Street, we saw this group of white boys again, maybe ten of them. They was running around and wrestling with each other and showing out. I remember we stopped and talked about going back to school, but then decided to go ahead, because there were lots of cars around and we didn't think they'd do anything. Well, about the time we got near the tracks they saw us and they quit their jumping around and stood for awhile. None of them said anything. We kept walking. Then one of them yelled something about the "little white nigger." I was scared to death then. Diane kept looking straight ahead and I did, too. But one of them boys said, "Hey! Where y'all goin' with that white nigger?" And the other ones started laughing and hollering at us.

So Diane looked at them and said, "You talkin' to us?" And one of them, a bigger one, says, "Who you *think* we're talkin' to?"

So she doesn't say nothing more. But I says, "We just walkin' this here boy home." I was hoping when they heard that they'd go on and leave us alone. But they hollered some more and it scared the boy and he took my hand. There was nothing for me to do but hold it. So there was quiet for awhile. Then a shout. And something hit on the ground beside me.

"They throwin' rocks!" Diane said.

All of a sudden they all picked up rocks from the railroad bed and started throwing. I remember closing my eyes and ducking, then grabbing the boy's hand tighter and pulling him as I started running as hard as I could go. And Diane was running and keeping her books up over her head to keep from getting hit. We ran across the street without even looking for cars and kept going down Jeff Davis. These boys chased us part of the way. I don't know when they stopped throwing and turned around, because I never looked back until we were part way up Sylvan. Ahead of us at the church there were some people and I knew we were safe. Diane stopped because some of them asked why we were running—and I think the boy was crying— but I kept going on to the house.

My mother was in the kitchen and she looked at me and says, "What in the world? Why you breathin' so fast like that?"

And as I told her about what happened it made me scared and mad at the same time, and I started crying and walking around the kitchen and living room and saying that if I had been a boy I'd have picked up some rocks myself and thrown them back.

Diane and the boy came in then and everyone was talking at once and I remember my mother listening to me and then putting her arms around me and patting me on the head. She tried to comfort me but I knew it made her nervous, because later she and the minister's wife went off to themselves and were talking about it and I could see they were worried.

I was so upset I went up to the bedroom and sat staring out the window. It wasn't fair them chasing us and throwing rocks at us. I knew why they had done it. It was because the boy's parents were civil-rights workers. To those white boys they were outsiders who had come here to cause trouble.

It was decided that day that we wouldn't walk to school anymore. After that the minister took us there and came to pick us up each afternoon.

The next day there was another incident which upset my mother. My older sisters, Nella and Alice, were coming home from Hudson High School with a group of other teenagers. They weren't doing anything, just coming home. They were four or five blocks from a demonstration. For some reason—and for no reason, really—a sheriff's car stopped and the deputies placed them all under arrest.

I didn't know anything about it until later that evening when my mother got a phone call. So she hangs up and says, ''They got Nella and Alice downtown. All

they was doin' was walkin' home. Jim Clark's got
'em." So she and my father and some other people
start out the door in a big hurry and I says, "I'm goin',
too." And my mother says, no, I'm to stay at home.
And she means inside, she says. "I don't want nothin'
else to happen. They got two already! You want 'em to
get you, too?"

So I waited there with Diane and Juliette and I just
couldn't understand it. I remember we'd always had
this statue of the Blessed Virgin Mary up on the wall
and I stood there and looked up at it and said to myself, I said, "How can all this be happenin' to us down
here? White boys throw rocks at us and nobody don't
do nothin' about it. And my sisters just come home,
just come walkin' home, and they get thrown in jail.
Boy, Mary, if we ever needed help down here, we
need it now."

My parents got Nella and Alice out on bond. I never
did know what they had been charged with.

A few days later, another sister, Charlene, who was
the second oldest, took part in a demonstration, was
arrested, and placed in a sweatbox (a small cubicle) at
the prison road camp. With all those things happening
at one time, it was understandable that my mother
might become depressed. But she never said anything
ill toward the whites or the sheriff. She got Charlene
out and that night we all went to the church, all seven
of us girls and our mother and when we started singing
the freedom songs all of us started clapping our hands
and smiling. I remember looking up at them and they

all looked so serene, yet determined. I think that was the only time we all sat together at a rally.

CHAPTER ELEVEN

Monday, February 1, 1965. Registration Day in Selma. Freedom Day some called it. Martin Luther King, Jr. returned to lead a march because this was one of only two days of the month that the registrar's office would be open. The march wouldn't reach the courthouse.

Sheyann

People began arriving at the church that morning very early, even though they knew it would be ten o'clock or so before the march began. I remember being there for awhile, then going back to the house to eat some breakfast, something I rarely did.

When I got back, Dr. King was already inside; so were the people. I had started up the church steps when I noticed the sheriff's department car parked just down the street. I don't know why I did it—maybe it was just to show we weren't afraid—but I turned from the steps and walked down toward them. I walked by looking at the two men inside. A short way down the street, I stopped, then came back, walking slow, like I was checking them out the same way they were keeping an eye on us.

As I passed by them again one of them called to me. I stopped.

"Where you goin'?" he asked.

"Why?" I said.

"We was just wonderin'. If you're goin' to the church there I'd think twice about it." Then he laughed.

"What you mean?" I asked.

"You goin' in there?" he repeated.

"Yes, sir," I said. "I'm goin' in."

"Well," he said, still grinning at me, "we been told somebody may have put a bomb in there. If you go in, you might not come out. You oughta be in school."

I stood there staring at him for awhile. The way he was smiling made me think he might have been joking. But it was a terrible way to show his sense of humor. On the other hand, I couldn't be sure he wasn't serious. White folks always had a way of laughing at us when they talked in them days. So I stood there a bit longer looking at the church, trying to make up my mind.

If there was a bomb in there—well, I had thought about dying before. The more I thought about it, the more concerned I became. For a while I really thought about just going home. But when I looked at those deputies sitting there looking so amused with me, I knew I had to keep up a front. So I just sort of tossed my head around from them and walked as fast as I could, than ran up the steps and went inside. Common sense told me to go home, not to take a chance. But in those days, you couldn't always go by common sense.

There wasn't a bomb in there, and I don't know to

this day if there had even been a bomb threat called in, or whether that deputy just made it up. But I know when we came out for the march, I felt relieved to be out in the sunshine in one piece.

The march began and what made it different was the fact that we were massed together in the street; always before we had marched in twos or threes on the sidewalk. But this time we went right down the street, and we sang and clapped our hands and it was such a joyous thing. But when we turned down Alabama Avenue, there was Selma Public Safety Director Wilson Baker and some of the Selma police officers and they had the street blocked. I was about halfway back in the march and couldn't hear what was said between Dr. King and Baker. But Baker wouldn't let us go on without a parade permit. And Dr. King, I was told later, just kept insisting that "I gotta keep on." And Baker asked him three times not to do it. And each time Dr. King would tell him we had to keep on. So Baker said we were under arrest and we all followed him on to the city hall.

I remember, there were so many of us that we formed a half circle in front. Nobody appeared worried about being put in jail; most were in a jubilant mood. Some of us started singing and Baker stood up there patiently, watching us and every once in a while trying to say something. Finally, we stopped and he told us that if we didn't know why we were being arrested, we were free to go. Some of the people left.

The rest of us stood by, waiting. Again Baker told us we could go. It came down to the fact that anyone who didn't want to be jailed, didn't have to be.

So they put Dr. King and Dr. Abernathy and about two hundred and fifty others in jail and the rest of us went back to the church. I really didn't have a choice because some women said they needed me and some of the others to go back to help prepare for the rally that night. I wanted to stay. And I remember stopping and looking back and watching Dr. King and Dr. Abernathy talking there along side of the building with Baker. I don't believe the police would have jailed me anyway.

The arrest and jailing of Martin Luther King, Jr. created a new sense of uneasiness among the white citizens of Selma, most of whom kept up with the marches and demonstrations only through news reports; a few went downtown for the daily confrontation, but most went about their business as usual.

Sheyann

I think what the people of Selma, the white people, feared more than anything was the time when a large number of children would begin marching. I think they feared that Jim Clark would react with anger and we'd really bring about national interest in Selma and give the city a worse image than it already had.

On February the third, that time arrived. After school that day, about three hundred students—most of them junior-high kids who were older than me—

gathered at the church, began singing songs, and then started to march to the city hall.

They carried signs about having the right to vote and about getting Dr. King out of jail. I went with them, and before we got to the city hall Mr. Baker got in front of us and announced that it was "time for you to go home." He kept repeating that he didn't want us to be in trouble, that he wanted us to go home.

Every time he'd say something, we'd listen, then start singing again. So, finally, he announced that we were all to follow him, that we were under arrest. Everybody was laughing and clapping their hands then, and walked down the street behind him. They took our names down as we passed by the desk, and some of us were then told to go home. The others were jailed.

The church rallies were held each evening, and the crowds, it seemed, gradually grew in number.

What I remember also about that part of the movement—early February—was that the rains began. Hardly a day went by, it seems, that there wasn't some rain. It would get worse.

I think my parents remember more vividly than me, but it was also the time I was becoming more insistent that they join the marches.

I remember my daddy sometime just getting up and walking out of the kitchen when I'd start. But my mother would listen as she always did—and agree with me. I remember once she told me that I was really growing up fast, and even seemed to know more about what was going on than she did.

Still, they put me off. They'd attend the rallies to listen to me and Rachel sing, but they'd never join the marches.

Dr. King stayed in the jail a few days and returned to the church one afternoon. I remember Rachel was there—she must have left school early—and she and I were standing together when he arrived. And everybody applauded him and then began singing *We Shall Overcome.*

Just seeing him there, I think, gave us another boost.

CHAPTER TWELVE

The efforts of blacks in Selma triggered civil-rights activities in adjoining counties. In Marion, twenty-eight miles away, Perry County Sheriff William Loftis arrested three hundred blacks, most of them youngsters, as they marched to the courthouse. New marches were planned. Governor George Wallace, watching developments in the simmering Black Belt, dispatched more state troopers.

Rachel

Like most little girls, Shey and I used to like to go walking. We'd put our arms around each other's shoulders and walk along, talking about things like what we would do when we grew up, getting married, having babies and all that, you know. Even when this historic civil-rights thing was going on, we still took time off to get away from the other children and just wander off alone. If we felt like going to the church and watching what was going on there, we'd do it. If we wanted to go to a store, we'd do that, even though we usually had no money.

Well, one day this priest gave us a half-dollar each. Boy did we think we were something. We headed for the little store nearby to get us some orange drink.

So we were walking and talking about babies. I wanted a boy and a girl, and she said something about maybe just having a little girl someday, so she could dress her up like a doll.

Well, for some reason—and maybe it was because of the things that were happening in our lives—we got started talking about dying and what happens when you die.

"I guess your soul just gets up and flies away like a bird," I said.

Shey didn't know about that. It might take a bit longer, she said, before your soul departs the earth.

Well, I really didn't know, I told her. But it seemed likely to me that the soul just lifted straight up to Heaven, if that's where you were going.

But Shey said she thought maybe you stayed around for awhile to meet some of the others who had gone before—the other relatives, the people who had been slaves.

Well, it was something to think about. Maybe that did happen, I said. And we kept walking and thinking and talking about it, because we feared that sooner or later it might happen.

Dr. Martin Luther King, Jr., during a rainy Selma demonstration in February, 1965.

A Dallas County deputy sheriff uses his nightstick to keep blacks in line during a voter-registration attempt in February, 1965.

"The thing that scares me," I said, "is that some-body might come by sometime and just shoot at us and hit us."

It scared her, too. She had been told that bullets burn you when they hit. But we kept wondering about the soul, and we finally concluded that maybe some of your relatives from earlier times came down to get you and led you back up to Heaven. And the times being as they were, we figured that maybe you'd march up there, past the clouds and the lightning, on up past the sun.

And we stopped and looked up at the sky and I said, "Boy, Shey, that'd be *some* march."

And we figured that once you did get up there the Lord would greet you and say your name and tell you, "Sheyann Webb, or Rachel West, you free girl. Yes, ma'am, you free!"

We thought about it for a long time that day. I didn't know what Sheyann was thinking, but however it was when your time was up, I wasn't in a big hurry to find out.

We talked about a lot of things as we grew up in those troubled times. But in the events that came, it had a significance, because there were times when we both thought we might be killed.

One afternoon [February 10] I was sitting on the church steps watching some of the smaller children play a game of kickball. I hadn't gone to the downtown because I was kept in the house by my mother, who got after me about doing my homework. There was a march of some kind that day, with mostly teenagers taking part.

So I was sitting there and I heard people shouting, all excited about something. I jumped up and saw several girls and boys running through the complex yard across the street from the church, on the side toward Clark School.

People were coming out of the apartments and running to them; I hurried across the street, arriving in time to see one of the boys bend over and vomit.

Everybody was talking at once, trying to find out what had happened, and a bigger girl, trying to catch her breath and talk, said that they had been in front of the courthouse and Sheriff Clark had come out and shouted, "Left face," and they all turned, and then he shouted, "March!" So they started to march, thinking they were going to jail. But the deputies pushed them and prodded them with their clubs, making them run toward the prison road camp about five miles away.

"We was run out of town," the girl said. "And when we dropped out to catch our wind they's get after us and threaten to hit us. They kept saying, 'You wanted to march, so march!' They wouldn't let us rest."

Others were straggling in, and some of them vomited. I watched with wide eyes. They had been made to run until they were sick.

Finally, after several miles, the deputies let them go,

apparently sure they'd worn all the "marching fever" out of them.

"We gonna march again!" the girl was shouting. "He ain't gonna stop us. He ain't!"

Sheriff Clark's tactics angered the black community. Some students of the civil-rights movement believe that the voting-rights drive in Selma may have been losing much of its steam, so much so, in fact, that the SCLC was looking for another town in the Black Belt to put some new life into its efforts. But Sheriff Jim Clark came through for the movement in Selma. He gave it just the spark it needed when he force-marched the black teenagers.

Rachel

We were after Jim Clark, then. We knew we couldn't let go. Well, it must have gotten to him. I don't know. But on the twelfth day of February, the news was going around that he had suffered a heart attack. We didn't know for sure, so some of the leaders checked it out and found he had been put in a hospital with chest pains. I remember thinking that maybe the Lord, somehow, had decided to do something and maybe had hit Jim Clark with that attack.

So a bunch of us gathered—this was on a Friday, I think—and we went down to the courthouse. Me and Shey went there and we carried signs that said we wanted Jim Clark well. And we knelt down there in front and we prayed for him. We wanted him and all the other whites in Selma to know we were not mad at him, that we wanted him to be well and that we knew the Lord was on our side. Even though we had been wronged by him, and by them [the whites] for all those years, we wanted them to know we were still willing to forgive them. I think it may have affected some of the white people. But others got mad, I'm sure, saying we were just "putting on an act." But that wasn't so. I remember kneeling there, and when I prayed for Jim Clark I really meant it.

I know some of the deputies were glaring at us, that day; they didn't believe us. They thought we were mocking them. But when we prayed for something it wasn't a joke. See, in those days we didn't have much at all. Really, about the only thing we had was our churches and our prayers. It wasn't done for a show. I know I wasn't there just because there were photographers and television cameramen. I'd have gone there if nobody was there, because when you get into a person's religion, that's a serious thing. We didn't joke with the Lord. We weren't out there joking about our freedom, either, because that's what it was all about. Our freedom. And our best weapon was getting down and praying or standing up there and singing our hearts out. So that's what we did, and Sheriff Jim Clark just never could deal with it.

James Clark's chest pains turned out to be a bad case of indigestion. He emerged from the hospital wearing a suit with a lapel badge with the word *never* on it. "Negroes will never overcome us," he told newsmen.

CHAPTER THIRTEEN

The second February registration day was Monday the fifteenth. Again, as on the first, several hundred marched to the courthouse. Among them were Sheyann Webb's parents, John and Betty Webb.

Sheyann

My birthday was coming up on Wednesday, February the seventeenth, and I would be nine. I remember my momma asking me what I wanted (and she quickly reminded me to make it a moderate request, since money was tight) and I told her I didn't want any toys. So she asked again, and I said more than anything I wanted her and Daddy to join the marches and try to register.

"We ain't never gonna be free, Momma, if we don't all march," I told her.

She hadn't answered but later asked me again what I wanted, and I said that I had already told her what I wanted.

But the night before registration, that Sunday night, after the rally, Momma had kicked her shoes off and sat in the living room. Albert had fallen asleep on the couch, with his head in her lap. Daddy was seated in the chair. I was on the floor. So Momma said something about the march, asked him if he wanted to go with the people. And he didn't answer.

So she said, "Shey's been gettin' out there every day

with them people and she wants us to try. I think maybe she's right about it. I think she knows more about this than we do."

So he shook his head.

I don't know what else was said, because I went up to bed. But next morning when I came downstairs I found both sitting in the kitchen. Usually, Daddy was gone when I come down, headed for work. I wondered, was I up early?

"What time they marchin'?" my daddy asked.

It was so strange the way he said it, and I knew that he and Momma were going to go that day. I looked at Momma and she had a resigned expression on her face, but her eyes seemed to laugh. And she said, "Shey, you gettin' your birthday present a little early."

I nodded. Then I hugged them both. I was so proud of them.

It was late in the morning—maybe ten-thirty or so—when the march started. It was an exciting thing; I walked between my parents, holding their hands, and we sang all the way down there.

But the jubilation soon began to diminish as we stood and stood. The line moved at a crawl. At noon, some of the courthouse workers came out, and I remember some white women going by and spraying Raid insecticide and another can of some kind of disinfectant toward us; they wrinkled up their noses like we were smelly things. I remember my momma's eyes got wide and her mouth was set in a tight line, like she wanted to shout at them, but some of the march lead-

ers were walking up and down the line telling us to
stay calm. So we started singing again.

We stayed there until late in the afternoon, and
when Momma and Daddy got in they were told they
couldn't be registered that day but were given a
number which, they were told by the man in the office, would "hold" their place the next registration
day.

It was a disappointment to all of us. But as we hurried home Momma was saying she didn't care how
long it took, she was going to be back each day
they held registration until she could vote. She was
now determined. She had known of the way our
people had been treated; this was the first time she
had experienced it herself.

And when I say we hurried home, I mean it. Standing there all day was not only a challenge of our resolve to be full citizens, but also was an endurance
test of our bladders.

In later years, when we talked about that day,
Momma would say that it was my part in the drive that
inspired her and Daddy to join it. I remember I had,
several nights before that march, stayed up and shined
my daddy's shoes.

As I look back, it must have been a symbolic ges-
ture, really, making sure his "marching shoes" looked
their best.

The really strange thing about that particular time is
that I don't remember much at all about my birthday

itself. Most girls might have some recollection of their ninth birthday. But at the time there were so many things going on—important things in my life—that something like a birthday was trivial.

I think my mother baked a cake. I don't remember; neither does she. I say she must have only because she always had before then and did in the years after.

The day itself was like many others; it had rained. And before going into the church that night for a rally, Rachel and some other kids had chased me to impose the happy-birthday spanking, but she never caught up with me before I got inside.

CHAPTER FOURTEEN

February 18, 1965. Selma was relatively quiet, but in Marion, the seat of Perry County, where hundreds of blacks had been arrested earlier, there was word of another march in the offing. State troopers were summoned from over central Alabama, and by late afternoon a convoy of trooper vehicles sped through Selma en route to Perry County. That night, in Marion, about four hundred blacks gathered at the Zion Methodist Church, across the street from the town's picturesque white courthouse. After a rally of about two hours duration, they came out and were met by the troopers; a bloody confrontation ensued. Lights on the street corner were shot out by white bystanders, newsmen were beaten, and cameras were destroyed or sprayed with black paint. A black woodcutter, Jimmie Lee Jackson, was shot in the stomach by a trooper and later died. What happened in Marion, Alabama, that night was never seen by the world; so far as is known, not a single still picture or an inch of television news footage recorded these events.

Rachel

The civil-rights workers who were staying with us were still awake when some people got back from Marion with the news of what had happened. When the knock came, I was asleep; it woke me up. I remember everybody was talking about Marion. So they hurried and got their coats and left. At first I thought they were going there, but then my mother and father got their coats. I asked where they were going and they said to the church. This must have been at eleven at night, maybe later, I don't know. But I hurried and got dressed and got my coat and ran out into the darkness, following after them.

Now this wasn't any kind of planned rally, it was just something that seemed instinctive. We were drawn to that church because of the bad thing that had taken place at Marion. And as late as it was, I saw people hurrying through the cool night, all huddled together to keep warm, all coming to the church. There must have been fifty or sixty. Some of the leaders were up on the steps—the Reverend L.L. Anderson, the Reverend F.D. Reese, and Hosea Williams were up there. At that time I didn't know what had happened, but I knew it must have been bad, because the men were very worried looking and some of the women were crying.

So one of the ministers—it must have been Reese, I think—began telling about the incident. And others would add things as they went along and the people kept interrupting.

So Reese was talking about how the people came out of the church at Marion and were standing there and the trooper came up and told them to disperse:

"So they knelt down to pray," he said. "And this trooper hit one of them and the other troopers just rushed forward and began using their clubs."

"My, Lord," some of the people said. "They started beating them and all they was doin' was prayin'?"

And Reese says, "And then there was more beating, and the people became frightened and tried to get back inside the church, but they couldn't because there were still people in the doorway. So they ran and the troopers chased them, swinging at them with their clubs."

A reporter would say later that there was a distinct *popping* sound as clubs struck skulls.

Many were injured and bleeding, Anderson said. He said he had talked by phone with some of the Marion people.

"And who was shot?" an old man asked. "We heard a young man was shot."

And Anderson says it was a guy named Jimmie Lee Jackson. And everybody just starts talking at once, back and forth, you know. We all wanted to find out what had happened. And it goes like this:

Somebody says, "Who was it?"

And somebody says again, "Jimmie Jackson."

So some woman cries out, you know, "Oh, my God, I knowed him!"

And others say, real excited like, "I knowed him, too. Oh, God!"

So they want to know why he was shot and Reese and Anderson tell them about the beating and how Jimmie Jackson was at this café and saw his grandfather come in with his head bleeding. So he wants to take him to a doctor, but the troopers won't let him out. And they push him inside and hit him. And as they tell the story, the people with us are saying, "Oh, my God, they hit him," and things like that.

Well, the story goes on, how Jimmie Jackson's mother, whose name is Viola Jackson, comes and pushes a trooper who has been beating Jimmie.

"And the trooper hit her," Reese says.

And the people are excited and some of them say, "Oh, no, they hit his mother! Oh, God have mercy!" and "Lord, Lord!"

So Reese tells how the trooper then picked up Jimmie Jackson off the floor, shoved him against the wall, then shoots him in the stomach.

And again the people are all shaking their heads and saying, "Oh, God have mercy," and some are crying.

It was like a bad dream out there in the darkness. And sometime when the talking was going on

Sheyann and her mother came. Sheyann was as sleepy as I was. And then she nudged me, and asks, "Who they shoot? Who was it?"

"Jimmie Lee Jackson," I said

And Sheyann's eyes grew wider and she put a hand to her mouth. "Jimmie Lee Jackson!" she says. "I knowed him."

Well, this whole thing scared me. We had talked about death, but now it had happened, and even though it was in Marion, not Selma, it was still a part of our movement.

I shook my head slowly. "Shey," I said, "This is real bad. If they can shoot somebody over there, they can shoot somebody here."

In my mind, I viewed what might happen here the next time there was a demonstration: If there was shooting, if there was a bomb set someplace, who would it be that the people would gather at the church for? Who would it be the next time?

We stayed in the church a long time that night, even after the talking stopped. It was silent. We just stood there, waiting for some further word.

Later there would be more news coming in. We were told that Jackson had been taken to the hospital at Marion but was refused admittance. So he was brought, bleeding, to Good Samaritan in Selma.

Through the rainy week that followed, Rachel and Sheyann were at the church during daytime prayer vigils for Jimmie Lee Jackson.

After that night, the mood of the movement was more subdued. People were scared. I know I was. I kept thinking about what it would be like to get shot, how it must burn you inside. And I thought about that talk Shey and I had about what happens to your soul. We began noticing the trooper cars coming by, as we stood out there in front of the church singing, and

Sheyann and Rachel join hands with other demonstrators in a street meeting near the church. [courtesy of The Birmingham News]

each time I'd see them my heart would race a bit faster. It was a frightening time in which to live.

On February 25, 1965, early in the morning, Jimmie Lee Jackson's heart rate became erratic. He died before the sun rose.

I remember hearing the news on the radio when I got up that morning. I didn't know Jimmie Jackson, but he was one of us. I remember, after hearing that news report, going over to the front window and just staring outside. I wondered if I could go to another rally or demonstration. I wondered if I could even go outside again.

At school that day I remember the nuns led us in a prayer for Jimmie Jackson's soul and also to ask the Lord's help for the people of Selma. I remember I closed my eyes tight and prayed harder than I had ever prayed before. I needed help because I was scared.

That Saturday, it was two days after he had died, there was a memorial for Jimmie Jackson at the Brown Chapel AME Church, and me and Shey and some other children held candles. The ceremony was held outside on the steps. When we sang *O Freedom*, some of the people began to weep. And when it reached the part,

And before I'll be a slave
I'll be buried in my grave
And go home to my Lord
And be free

I was crying, too.

CHAPTER FIFTEEN

Two funeral services were held for Jimmie Lee Jackson, one at Brown Chapel in Selma, the other at Zion Methodist in Marion. It was a bleak day, and by the time the second service began the skies had exploded a chill, steady rain on the more than three thousand mourners. It was March 3, Ash Wednesday.

Sheyann

I had met Jimmie Lee Jackson only once. It was one night at Brown Chapel, and he had come there with Albert Turner, one of the SCLC workers from Marion. I remember I was with my daddy that night and we had talked briefly with them.

On the day of the funeral, my daddy and momma stayed home from work so they could attend. I remember the services vividly.

The Reverend L.L. Anderson gave the Selma eulogy, and he said that now Jimmie Lee Jackson "had earned his place in history beside John Brown, Abraham Lincoln, and Medger Evers. When Jimmie Lee Jackson gets up to Heaven, he won't find that God had one place for white people and another for black people, but just one place for all of us. Jimmie Lee Jackson's struggle is over, and he is free at last."

I remember his mother sat in the front, and her face still had bruise marks from when she had been hit by the trooper. She sat there crying. We sang several songs then, and one of them was *God Will Take Care of You*, and I remember some big lady sitting back about midway in the pews standing and crying out, "I *know* God will take care of me, I *know* He will!"

On this day, Momma had let Albert stay home from school, and he and Daddy and I went to Marion for the services there. We couldn't get inside at Zion because it was so crowded. The rain had just begun; it fell lightly through most of the service. Dr. King spoke and said Jimmie Lee Jackson had been murdered by the "brutality of every sheriff who practiced lawlessness in the name of the law . . . by every politician who fed his constituency the stale bread of hatred . . . by the timidity of a federal government that is willing to spend millions a day to defend freedom in Vietnam but cannot protect the rights of its citizens at home . . . and he was murdered by the cowardice of every Negro who passively accepts the evils of segregation and stands on the sidelines in the struggle for justice."

He told us we must not be bitter, that we must not lose faith in our white brothers. "Love will conquer hate," he said. "Truth, crushed into the earth, will rise again."

By the time we started the march to Heard Cemetery —and it was more than three miles away—the rain was falling in sheets. I didn't have an umbrella. My bonnet became sopped with water; my shoes were soaked. And what I remember so vividly was my daddy's blue suit. He had bought it several days before, and it wasn't very expensive. The blue color faded all into his white shirt.

There had been a lot of Selma people in Marion that

day. I knew it was important for us to be there, because it showed that blacks were standing together, no matter where they lived. Marion had been the "second front" in this battle for our freedom, but what had happened here had been worse than anything that had taken place in Selma. I remember a man from Marion talking to Daddy, and he was saying that Sheriff Jim Clark had been there the night of the beating.

When we marched through the rain behind Jimmie Lee Jackson's casket that day, we were letting the white people there know we were not afraid of their clubs or their guns. I'm sure Colonel Al Lingo, who led the troopers that night, felt that by giving us a good whipping he could put a stop to the marches and demonstrations. He was so wrong.

I remember thinking that maybe we had won something there, because nobody bothered us when we marched that day, and I thought maybe the whites were ashamed of what had happened.

But when we got home I later learned that some troopers stopped the car Dr. King was in as he returned to Selma. They had been waiting for him and gave Hosea Williams, who was driving, a ticket for speeding and reckless driving. I believed it was just a harassment tactic.

The rain had left me chilled to the bone, and I took a hot bath when I got home. Then I went over to Rachel's. Her mother had some rice made, and we sat on the living room floor while we ate a bowl of it.

I think the shooting death had a sobering effect on

all the people during that time; I believe a lot of people feared that something worse might happen. I know it bothered me; it bothered Rachel.

After we had finished the rice we walked over to the church and stood in the back.

We had been there several minutes when Rachel whispered, "Shey, you think Jimmie Jackson's up there yet?"

"I think he be there by now," I said. "You?"

She shrugged. "I think he is."

The next day Dr. King left Selma; he was to speak somewhere and go to Washington. I remember he told us that he had mentioned us to President Johnson and said he was proud of us.

It wasn't until later that day that I heard the news that a march had been called for that Sunday, from Selma to Montgomery. It was to protest police brutality at Selma and Marion as well as denial of voting rights all over the Black Belt.

At first, it didn't seem to cause much excitement. I remember telling Momma of the plans and she said for me not to worry about it, because she wasn't letting me march fifty miles.

CHAPTER SIXTEEN

March 6, 1965, a Saturday. Spring was beginning to emerge over the browned fields of the Black Belt. Jonquils nodded, puffs of forsythia sparkled on the horizon like golden, fine-spun cotton candy. But this year the changing seasons were of little concern to the people who lived at the George Washington Carver Homes in Selma.

Rachel

That Saturday was when I really began to get frightened about the march. I had gone over to the church and across the street, across Sylvan Street there, in the other yards. There were some people, some doctors and nurses from New York or someplace, and they were having this course for us. There were also some of our people, the SCLC people, there.

Well, the doctors said something about tear gas, about what to do when it was used. They said it would rise a little, so our best way to get away from it was to get low. They said get down on your knees and touch your face to the ground, and let the gas rise or go above you.

I remember watching them and even joining in the demonstrations, dropping to my knees and touching my nose to the ground. Over and over we'd do it. And we'd form a tight circle, women and children on the inside, with the men on the outside to protect us from the lawmen and their clubs. We would kneel there and put our hands over our heads.

I think what bothered me so much about it was that we'd never had anything like this before, no training. So I could only imagine that somebody was sure there'd be trouble, especially after what had happened over in Marion.

The day before, the place had been full of rumors. Some said there was going to be a march, others saying no, because Dr. King wasn't here. It was going back and forth like that, and we didn't know what to think. But that Saturday morning we got the news reports on radio from Montgomery that Governor Wallace was not allowing us to march and was going to use the state troopers to stop us. Well, that made some of the people even more determined.

I remember seeing Sheyann outside in the yard that afternoon and talking about what might lie ahead. And I asked her, "Shey, you gonna march tomorrow?"

And she shrugged. "I don't know, Rachel. You gonna march?"

I shook my head. "I don't know, Shey. I'm scared, to tell you the truth. Them people's training for tear gas. I don't want to get tear-gassed. I'm scared the same thing's gonna happen here that happen over in Marion. It really scares me."

She had stood there with her arms folded, I remember, and bit her lip while she thought about it. Then she told me what she had heard from some people who had been at the doctor's office that morning. A group of old women, she said, had sat in the waiting room and were crying.

"Cryin'?" I said. "Why they be cryin'?"

"My momma say they cryin' because they be scared of somethin' bad gonna happen here. She say them old women usually know."

The thought of the women crying added to my worries.

Incredibly, neither of the two chief adversaries in the civil-rights struggle in Alabama—Governor George Wallace and Dr. Martin Luther King, Jr.—seemed to be much concerned about the proposed march to Montgomery. They both thought it would be little more than a token effort. Neither expected it to become a major event in the civil-rights movement.

In Montgomery on March 5, a Friday, Governor Wallace at first agreed to provide trooper escort for the marchers. According to an administrative assistant, Cecil Jackson, a Selma attorney: "We felt that only a few hundred would try it and [that] most would give up after a few miles. But later, State Representative Bill Edwards of Lowndes County convinced the governor that snipers might be a problem and asked him to block the march. Finally the governor agreed to ban the march."

Meanwhile, Martin Luther King, Jr., and his top aide, the Reverend Ralph Abernathy, had returned to Atlanta for Lenten services, that Sunday being the first of the Easter season.

"Martin didn't really think the people were up to walking fifty miles," Abernathy would say later, in an August 1978 interview. "We thought it would be a routine march. But on that Sunday morning I got a call from [Hosea] Williams and he said there were 'thousands' ready to march. I couldn't believe it. So I called Martin and he was surprised, but he said to call back to Selma and tell them to go ahead and march as long as they were certain there'd be no trouble. And we were sure there wouldn't be."

Cecil Jackson, meanwhile, summoned officers of the state troopers to the governor's office. "We told them how to hold their clubs. We said they could stop the first ranks, turn them around, and the others would follow."

Jackson said plans were made to keep the hot-tempered Alabama Public Safety Director Al Lingo and Sheriff Jim Clark out of Selma. Clark was in Washington appearing on ABC Television's "Issues and Answers." He was to fly back to Montgomery, where Lingo was to pick him up. "He was told," Jackson said, "to keep Clark at the airport until the march was over."

This order was ignored. Lingo and Clark hurried from the airport to Selma, arriving moments before the marchers appeared at the Edmund Pettus Bridge.

And so, with the leaders thinking little of it, the stage was set for what would be known ever after as Bloody Sunday.

CHAPTER SEVENTEEN

Sunday, March 7, 1965. It was a breezy, mild day with blotches of purple-blue clouds scudding across the sky, partly obscuring the sun.

Overlooking downtown Selma, the Edmund Pettus Bridge seemed to lift in an obtrusive hump of flat-silver girding, then arched over the Alabama River. It measured three-tenths of a mile, most of it constructed of dingy brown concrete. It looked like so many other bridges in America.

When Sheyann Webb and Rachel West arose that morning they couldn't know that it would be on this day that Selma would take its place in the history books—alongside such places as Concord, Lexington, and Gettysburg—as a crucial battleground in a people's pursuit of freedom.

Sheyann

What woke me was the car horns blowing out on Sylvan Street, and people shouting. Albert Turner, I discovered later, had led about three hundred people from Perry County and they were ready to march to Montgomery. I hadn't slept well that night; I'd had a stomach ache, which my mother said was caused by worry.

She had sat up with me the night before, telling me that if I didn't feel well I didn't have to march. In fact, she was hoping I wouldn't. I would hear talk in later years that there had been uncertainty about whether there would even be a march. But I had never been told about it. All I knew was that there were plans for it, and I knew I belonged there with the people. It was important that I try to go with them to Montgomery in hopes of seeing Governor Wallace and telling him we wanted the right to vote, the right to be free. That's all I knew.

So I got up and put on a dress and went downstairs and asked my momma to fix my hair. I remember she looked at me rather strangely for a moment, then turned me around while she brushed it. There had been talk that morning, she said, of state troopers pulling a black man from his car and whipping him. It frightened her; it frightened me. The troopers, she said, were all over town.

"You want me to stay home?" I asked her.

She kept brushing for awhile, then said, "I want you to do what you know is right."

Well, I was going to march, I told her. So she nodded, and all of a sudden she hugged me close to her, then turned away.

"Momma," I said, "you gonna cry?"

And she shook her head. "No, I'm just proud of you," she said, but she was wiping at her eyes. So I went and hugged her once real quick, then left for the church. The march was supposed to begin at noon.

It would be well after the noon hour before a march was undertaken. Inside the church, Hosea Williams, Andrew Young, John Lewis, and Albert Turner thrashed out the idea with Selma's

"Bloody Sunday." March 7, 1965. The march across the Edmund Pettus Bridge begins, with Hosea Williams and John Lewis (in raincoat, far right) forming the front rank. Albert Turner (in white cap), who had brought marchers from Perry County, is seen just to the rear of Williams. This photo and others in sequence, were taken by Tom Lankford for *The Birmingham News*. [courtesy of *The Birmingham News*]

The marchers are met by gas-masked state troopers, who begin to advance. [courtesy of *The Birmingham News*]

The wedge of troopers pushes and turns the first rank. [courtesy of *The Birmingham News*]

In a sudden lurching movement, the lawmen ram forward, knocking marchers about like tenpins. [courtesy of *The Birmingham News*]

In the aftermath, a marcher lies injured on the curb, while a trooper runs to the rear and mounted possemen prepare to surge forward. [courtesy of *The Birmingham News*]

Rifle-toting troopers sweep triumphantly by Brown Chapel where some of the marchers sought shelter. [courtesy of *The Birmingham News*]

Reverend F.D. Reese, Reverend Lorenzo Harrison, and Reverend L.L. Anderson and others. Turner was determined to march, "even if it's just around the church. I got the people here," he said, "and if we don't march, they'll feel let down." After calling Atlanta and talking with King and Abernathy, it was decided that the march would be held as announced. Williams and Young flipped a coin to see who would lead it. Williams lost. He and John Lewis of the Student Nonviolent Coordinating Committee, would walk in front. Turner would be in the second rank, with Jim Mantz. Early in the afternoon the column left Brown Chapel AME Church and proceeded up Sylvan Street, where it was met by Selma Public Safety Director Wilson Baker. He ordered the marchers to return to the church. An hour later, just before two o'clock, a second march began. Baker didn't stop it. It moved, six-hundred strong, through the downtown, then turned south, toward the bridge over the Alabama River.

Sheyann

I was walking between some young white guy and a black woman; I think she must have been from Perry County. Before we had left the church we had sung *Ain't Gonna Let Nobody Turn Me 'Round* and several other songs, but as we got to the downtown and started toward the bridge we got quiet. I think we stopped for just a short time there, and I was told later some of the leaders talked about going another route—back through town and out State Highway 14—to get around the troopers who were across the bridge, on the side toward Montgomery. I don't know what was said for sure, but after just a little while we started again.

Now the Edmund Pettus Bridge sits above the

downtown; you have to walk up it like it's a little hill. We couldn't see the other side, we couldn't see the troopers. So we started up and the first part of the line was over. I couldn't see all that much because I was so little; the people in front blocked my view.

But when we got up there on that high part and looked down we saw them. I remember the woman saying something like, "Oh, my Lord" or something. And I stepped out to the side for a second and I saw them. They were in a line—they looked like a blue picket fence—stretched across the highway. [Broad Street becomes United States Highway 80] There were others gathered behind that first line and to the sides, along the little service road in front of the stores and drive-ins, there was a group of white people. And further back were some of Sheriff Jim Clark's posse-men on their horses. Traffic had been blocked.

At that point I began to get a little uneasy about things. I think everyone did. People quit talking; it was so quiet then that all you could hear was the wind blowing and our footsteps on the concrete sidewalk.

Well, we kept moving down the bridge. I remember glancing at the water in the Alabama River, and it was yellow and looked cold. I was told later that Hosea Williams said to John Lewis, "See that water down there? I hope you can swim, 'cause we're fixin' to end up in it."

The troopers could be seen more clearly now. I guess I was fifty to seventy-five yards from them. They were wearing blue helmets, blue jackets, and they carried clubs in their hands; they had those gas-mask pouches slung across their shoulders. The first part of the march line reached them and we all came to a stop. For a few seconds we just kept standing, and then I heard this voice speaking over the bullhorn saying that this was an unlawful assembly and for us to disperse and go back to the church.

I remember I held the woman's hand who was next to me and had it gripped hard. I wasn't really scared at that point. Then I stepped out a way and looked again and saw the troopers putting on their masks. *That* scared me. I had never faced the troopers before, and nobody had ever put on gas masks during the downtown marches. But this one was different; we were out of the city limits and on a highway. Williams said something to the troopers asking if we could pray—I didn't hear it but was told later he asked if we could—and then I heard the voice again come over the bullhorn and tell us we had two minutes to disperse.

Some of the people around me began to talk then, saying something about, "Get ready, we're going to jail," words to that effect.

But I didn't know about that; the masks scared me. So the next thing I know—it didn't seem like two minutes had gone by—the voice was saying, "Troopers advance and see that they are dispersed." Just all of a sudden it was beginning to happen. I couldn't see for sure how it began, but just before it did I took another

look and saw the line of troopers moving toward us;
the wind was whipping at their pants legs.

The masked lawmen walked slowly forward, their clubs held
crossways, and pushed against Lewis and Williams. There was a
brief pause, then a sudden lunge forward. Lewis, wearing a white
raincoat and a backpack, toppled backward; then a club raised
and flashed as it came down, striking his head. A startled scream
filled the air. The troopers charged then, running and pushing
with their clubs; some swung them. The marchers turned and
began to run, their cries and instant retreat eliciting whoops of
glee from some of the white bystanders.

Sheyann

All I knew is I heard all this screaming and the people
were turning and I saw this first part of the line running
and stumbling back toward us. At that point, I was just
off the bridge and on the side of the highway. And
they came running and some of them were crying out
and somebody yelled, "Oh, God, they're killing us!" I
think I just froze then. There were people everywhere,
jamming against me, pushing against me. Then, all of
a sudden, it stopped and everyone got down on their
knees, and I did too, and somebody was saying for us
to pray. But there was so much excitement it never got
started, because everybody was talking and they were
scared and we didn't know what was happening or
was going to happen. I remember looking toward the
troopers and they were backing up, but some of them
were standing over some of our people who had been

knocked down or had fallen. It seemed like just a few seconds went by and I heard a shout. "Gas! Gas!" And everybody started screaming again. And I looked and I saw the troopers charging us again and some of them were swinging their arms and throwing canisters of tear gas. And beyond them I saw the horsemen starting their charge toward us. I was terrified. What happened then is something I'll never forget as long as I live. Never. In fact, I still dream about it sometimes.

I saw those horsemen coming toward me and they had those awful masks on; they rode right through the cloud of tear gas. Some of them had clubs, others had ropes or whips, which they swung about them like they were driving cattle.

I'll tell you, I forgot about praying, and I just turned and ran. And just as I was turning the tear gas got me; it burned my nose first and then got my eyes. I was blinded by the tears. So I began running and not see-ing where I was going. I remember being scared that I might fall over the railing and into the water. I don't know if I was screaming or not, but everyone else was. People were running and falling and ducking and you could hear the horses' hooves on the pavement and you'd hear people scream and hear the whips swish-ing and you'd hear them striking the people. They'd cry out; some moaned. Women as well as men were getting hit. I never got hit, but one of the horses went right by me and I heard the swish sound as the whip went over my head and cracked some man across the back. It seemed to take forever to get across the bridge.

It seemed I was running uphill for an awfully long time. They kept rolling canisters of tear gas on the ground, so it would rise up quickly. It was making me sick. I heard more horses and I turned back and saw two of them and the riders were leaning over to one side. It was like a nightmare seeing it through the tears. I just knew then that I was going to die, that those horses were going to trample me. So I kind of knelt down and held my hands and arms up over my head, and I must have been screaming—I don't really remember.

All of a sudden somebody was grabbing me under the arms and lifting me up and running. The horses went by and I kept waiting to get trampled on or hit, but they went on by and I guess they were hitting at somebody else. And I looked up and saw it was Hosea Williams who had me and he was running but we didn't seem to be moving, and I kept kicking my legs in the air, trying to speed up, and I shouted at him, "Put me down! You can't run fast enough with me!"

But he held on until we were off the bridge and down on Broad Street and he let me go. I didn't stop running until I got home. All along the way there were people running in small groups; I saw people jumping over cars and being chased by the horsemen who kept hitting them. When I got to the apartments there were horsemen in the yards, galloping up and down, and one of them reared his horse up in the air as I went by, and he had his mask off and was shouting something at me.

When I got into the house my momma and daddy

were there and they had this shocked look on their
faces and I ran in and tried to tell them what had
happened. I was maybe a little hysterical because I
kept repeating over and over, "I can't stop shaking,
Momma, I can't stop shaking," and finally she
grabbed me and sat down with me on her lap. But my
daddy was like I'd never seen him before. He had a
shotgun and he yelled, "By God, if they want it this
way, I'll give it to them!" And he started out the door.
Momma jumped up and got in front of him shouting at
him. And he said, "I'm ready to die; I mean it! I'm
ready to die!" I was crying there on the couch, I was
so scared. But finally he put the gun aside and sat
down. I remember just laying there on the couch, crying and feeling so disgusted. They had beaten us like
we were slaves.

CHAPTER EIGHTEEN

As the march began, Rachel West remained behind at the church
with some others, including Andrew Young, who were to try to
organize some logistical plan—food, water tenting, etc.—for the
march if it were allowed to proceed. Up to this point there had
been no such planning because, as Young would say later, no
one seriously believed that the march would get out of Selma.

Rachel

My father went with the march and I stayed out in
front of the church watching as they went toward the

downtown. I had asked my mother about going with
them but she had told me, no, we were staying back. I
remember seeing Sheyann earlier that day, but I didn't
know until later she was with them.

Well, we watched them leave, and I remember
thinking to myself that I should be with them. I really
wanted to go, even though I'll admit I was afraid.
There had been so many rumors flying around about
the chances of some real trouble. I knew I couldn't
walk fifty miles, and my mother knew she couldn't,
and she had said that if they got down the road toward
Montgomery apiece we might go over and join them
for part of the march later.

So I was standing there and the last of the people in
the march made the turn from Sylvan Street and dis-
appeared. I don't know what I was thinking about, but
I just started to follow them, taking a shortcut through
the apartment yards across Sylvan and running up toward the downtown area. There were several other
kids with me.

But we never got there. All of a sudden I heard
people screaming and shouting and I stopped to see
what was happening. I saw these people running from
all over the place, running toward me. They were
holding their arms up to their heads like bees were
after them or something. I knew something was
wrong, but I didn't know for sure what it was. But I just
went cold with fear because it was awful. There were
men, women, and some teenagers, and some of them
were tripping and stumbling. Then I saw the horsemen

behind them, riding at a gallop, coming around a house up the way, and that's when I turned and ran.

I heard the horses' hooves and I turned and saw the riders hitting at the people and they were coming fast toward me. I stopped and got up against the wall of one of the apartment buildings and pressed myself against it as hard as I could. Two horsemen went by and I knew if I didn't move I would be trapped there. I saw the people crying as they went by and holding their eyes and some had their arms up over their heads. I took off running.

Well, I started screaming and ran as hard as I could. When I was crossing Sylvan, I could see the church and there were people—those who had waited out front—and they were scattering in all directions.

I was out in the open then, right in the middle of the street and heading for the yard toward our house, and I heard these other horsemen coming and I knew they were going to catch me. I just knew they were going to either trample me or hit me with a club or whip. My legs didn't seem to be moving—it was like in a bad dream when you are chased by something and can't run. Well, just as I got to the yard this white guy named Frank Soracco came by me and he was moving fast. And I must have been crying out because he stopped and just swept me up and carried me under the armpits and kept moving. There were people all around us and they were almost wild with fear, because this one horseman was right behind us, and there were several others coming on fast.

This white guy headed straight into our front door, dropped me, then ran up the steps to the bathroom and locked the door. My mother and some of my brothers and sisters were in the living room and the way they were breathing—real hard and fast— I knew that some of them had ran from the possemen. I know we were all scared to death. We didn't know where my father was.

I remember we hurried and locked the doors. I looked out the window and there were horsemen all over the place, riding back and forth—sort of prancing—across the yard. Most of the people were inside, either in some of the apartments or in the church. And in a little while we saw troopers walking through the yard and they carried rifles. They were like soldiers in a war zone, which was silly, because there hadn't been a battle. We hadn't fought them. It had been all one-sided. There had been women and children out there, and none of them had carried weapons. Some men did go out with shotguns, but Andrew Young and others told them to stay indoors. A few boys threw some rocks and bottles, but they were also told to go inside and they did. If people were mad, it was understandable.

It was maybe fifteen minutes or so after I got inside the house that I began to hear the sirens of ambulances wailing, coming for some of the injured people.

At the time we didn't know how many were hurt; we didn't know if some might have been killed. My father came in sometime before the troopers with the rifles walked through the complex, and he had told us there had been a number who had been injured. After things had settled down outside, my mother and I walked to the church to see what was going on. There were still some troopers standing down the street a ways, but the horsemen had retreated about two blocks away. An aid station had been set up in the parsonage of the church and some of the more badly injured people—they were bleeding, and some had to be carried on stretchers—were placed in ambulances and taken to hospitals. I saw a trooper help carry a man to an ambulance.

There were some people in the church. But when you looked across the yards or up and down the street you didn't see a black person anywhere. If they weren't in the church, they were in their homes with the doors locked. And some were at the hospital.

Later that evening we went back to the church. What I saw there I will always remember—the faces of the people. They were like masks. Some of them were still crying, but they all just sat there staring to the front. I had never seen such looks before. They were hurt, they were angry, they were outraged. The smell of tear gas was everywhere; it was in their clothes, in their hair. It stung my eyes.

And everything was so quiet. The only sound was the sobbing. We had really been hurt. The movement, I mean. There had never been a time like this. Nobody was praying, nobody was singing. They just sat and stared and cried. It seemed like all their eyes were glazed and glassy. I remember I just kept sitting there, looking at them. It really seemed then that we had lost everything we had fought for.

We must have sat there an hour. I remember Reverend Reese getting up and talking, and Hosea Williams also spoke. But no one seemed to listen. I think in that moment the will to go on was lost. I wondered if there would ever be another march.

I remember when Reverend Reese spoke that he said something about "vengeance is mine, saith the Lord." But he just quit talking after that. I think he said something about our dignity could never be crushed. But the people just kept staring, like they were looking at something beyond the church, not hearing the words.

Shey came in and sat down near me. I could see she was upset. Some of the people who had been hurt at the bridge, Mrs. Amelia Boynton and Mrs. Margaret Moore, came in, and their heads had bandages around them.

All the things that I had feared seemed to be coming true—the horsemen and the beatings. Now, all that was left was the bombing. But by then, seeing the faces of the people and listening to them cry made me so demoralized that I didn't even care anymore. It was dark outside and I felt there was more danger there than in the church. It might even have been safer than our home, because some of the white civil-rights workers were there and the horsemen were mad at them. They wanted to kill them, I was sure, especially the way they had chased the guy who carried me in. So the church was the place to be, I thought. So we just stayed there and we stared straight ahead. And we cried. It just seemed in that moment that everything was so hopeless. All we had in this whole world was just we, ourselves.

I didn't think that crying and sobbing was ever going to stop.

Finally, somebody gets up and says something about the way they had ridden down on us, like we were animals.

Then it gets quiet again. Later, somebody else gets up and says something about "everybody had got to have a cross to bear, and that bridge was ours."

Then it got quiet again, and we just sat there. It was like no other church meeting I'd ever been to before.

CHAPTER NINETEEN

In the chill March night, state troopers waited at a road block about a block from the church, sealing off Sylvan Street and the black section of Selma from the rest of the world. Alabama Public Safety Director Al Lingo, who had—with Sheriff Clark—taken charge of the lawmen at the bridge that afternoon, told reporters that, for all practical purposes, "controlled force" had put an end to the demonstrations in Selma, just as it had done in Marion. As the troopers drank coffee and paced restlessly about, an eerie, bewildering silence hung over the street.

Sheyann

When I had first gotten to the church that night, my eyes were still swollen and burning from the tear gas. But what I saw there made me cry again. I'll never forget the faces of those people. I'd never seen such looks before. I remember standing and looking at them a long time before sitting down. They weren't afraid, because they were too beaten to know any more fear. It was as though nobody cared to even try to win anything anymore, like we were slaves after all and had been put in our place by a good beating.

I sat with Rachel up toward the front. Now there were a bunch of kids up there. So we were just sitting there crying, listening to the others cry; some were even moaning and wailing. It was an awful thing. It was like we were at our own funeral.

But then later in the night, maybe nine-thirty or ten, I don't know for sure, all of a sudden somebody there started humming. I think they were moaning and it just went into the humming of a freedom song. It was real low, but some of us children began humming along, slow and soft. At first I didn't even know what it was, what song, I mean. It was like a funeral sound, a dirge. Then I recognized it—*Ain't Gonna Let Nobody Turn Me 'Round*. I'd never heard it or hummed it that way before. But it just started to catch on, and the people began to pick it up. It started to swell, the humming. Then we began singing the words. We sang, "Ain't

gonna let George Wallace turn me 'round." And, "Ain't
gonna let Jim Clark turn me 'round." "Ain't gonna let
no state trooper turn me 'round."

Ain't gonna let no horses . . .ain't gonna let no tear
gas—ain't gonna let nobody turn me 'round. *Nobody!*
And everybody's singing now, and some of them
are clapping their hands, and they're still crying, but
it's a different kind of crying. It's the kind of crying
that's got spirit, not the weeping they had been doing.

And me and Rachel are crying and singing and it
just gets louder and louder. I know the state troopers
outside the church heard it. Everybody heard it. Because more people were coming in then, leaving their
apartments and coming to the church—because something was happening.

We was singing and telling the world that we hadn't
been whipped, that we had won.

*Just all of a sudden something happened that night
and we knew in that church that—Lord Almighty—we
had really won, after all. We had won!*

I think we all realized it at the same time, that we
had won something that day, because people were
standing up and singing like I'd never heard them before.

And Reverend Reese was up at the pulpit and he
announced that Dr. King had called and said he was
coming back the next day and he was bringing help
for us. Well, it was that night that the whole nation—
even the whole world—saw what had happened that
day in Selma. It hadn't been like in Marion; the television cameras had gotten the whole thing.

Reverend Reese said later that what happened at the church that night was the pivotal event in the voting-rights drive in Selma. Our nonviolent approach had been threatened, because so many people were angry and wanted to retaliate against the possemen and the troopers. If that had happened, our efforts to point out the injustice in Alabama might have been lost. If our people had allowed themselves to become common rioters, the sympathy we had gained from the days and days of marching would have been for nothing. After the beating at the bridge, we faced a crisis point in our movement. Despite what had been endured at the bridge and in the streets, we had to maintain our sense of dignity. We had to keep it.

When I first went into that church that evening those people sitting there were beaten—I mean their spirit, their will was beaten. But when that singing started, we grew stronger. Each one of us said to ourselves that we could go back out there and face the tear gas, face the horses, face whatever Jim Clark could throw at us.

It was very late when we went to bed that night. I was exhausted. But I kept waking up all through the night and seeing those horsemen coming toward me.

It had been a day and a night that none of us would ever forget.

The next day, Monday, March the eighth, people from all over the country—mostly ministers and some nuns—began arriving to help us. They were all over the apartment yards and at the church and we were asked—those who lived there—to provide room for them. I remember that very few of the children went to school that morning. They were running back and forth between Brown Chapel and their homes, helping the newcomers with their baggage and finding places for them to stay.

My mother stayed home and I was bringing some of the priests and ministers to the house, offering them our home to stay in. Before the middle of the afternoon there were twenty guests there, and Momma was busy fixing coffee in the kitchen.

So she stopped me as I was going out the back door and she whispered loudly, "Shey! Where you goin'?" And I told her to the church. And she said, "Well, you can't go bringin' nobody else here 'cause we ain't got no more room." She wasn't mad, just concerned about space. So I didn't ask anyone else over.

It was that way everyplace, folks just opening up their homes to the visitors who had come after seeing on television the way we had been beaten.

That night Dr. King came back and there was a rally at the church. There wasn't room for everyone inside. People were standing out in the street and there were loudspeakers set up so those on the outside could hear. When he first came in we sang *Battle Hymn of the Republic*, and everybody stood up.

When we finished he told us how proud he was of us, and then he asked the visiting ministers—who were all seated in a group toward the front—to stand

A line of deputies hems in civil-rights demonstrators near Brown Chapel in the wake of Bloody Sunday. [Selma Police Photo]

and introduce themselves. And each one would get up and say his name and tell us something like, "We've come to help."

"Thank God we're not alone," Dr. King would say.

We applauded each of them; we were grateful that we were not forgotten. But the loudest applause came when Dr. King announced that the next day he would lead another march back to the bridge. Everybody stood up because we were ready to go again. Some of the people were shouting that they were ready right then.

On that Tuesday, the ninth of March, more ministers were arriving. The yard of the George Washington
Carver Homes was full of people. Some stood in
groups and sang songs, the newly arrived ministers
holding hands with our people. One of them was the
Reverend James Reeb of Boston, a Unitarian. He was
one of many I invited to come by for coffee. I was
inviting all of them.

Early that afternoon about two thousand of us followed Dr. King to the bridge and across it. I didn't
know it for sure at the time, but a federal judge in
Montgomery, Frank M. Johnson, Jr., had issued an
order forbidding any further marches from Selma to
Montgomery until he held a hearing; but we went
anyway. The troopers were waiting again but this time
they stood back and waited while we had some
prayers and sang some songs. Then we turned around
and came back to the church. I was told later that Dr.
King hadn't planned on going to Montgomery, because Judge Johnson was going to have a hearing on
whether we could. But as we came back across the
bridge some young black men stood on a street corner
and sang, *Ain't Gonna Let Nobody Turn Me 'Round.*

Being a child, I naturally thought they were singing
that because they were on our side. Later I learned that
they were against Dr. King's nonviolent philosophy
and were really singing that to mock him. And to
mock us. We didn't need their kind of help.

When we got back to the church, we disbanded and
I went home. Now there were people everywhere and

I saw my momma outside the front door, and she was talking to these ministers, and I recognized them as a group I had invited over. Reverend Reeb was among them.

There wouldn't have been any special reason to remember him, I don't suppose, but for the fact that he would become one of the martyrs in the voting-rights drive. That afternoon, he said, he couldn't stay for coffee right then because he and some of the others were going downtown to eat.

But he promised he would come back later. He had not planned to stay very long in Selma, he said, but was changing his mind and might remain through the week.

Of course, he never did come back to my house. Returning to the church after eating at a black-owned restaurant, he and the others—it was three others— were attacked by some white men. One of them hit him with a club.

When we first heard the report that something had happened downtown, I didn't realize he was the one. But my mother had talked with some of the people and she came back to where I was in front of the church.

"Shey," she said, "you know who it was that got beat up?"

And I says, "Who it was?"

"That one with the glasses that was coming for coffee."

We didn't know how bad he was. But I remembered

that when he had been talking to us he had asked my momma if she had the kind of coffee with chicory in it. A lot of people in the South used chicory coffee, but Momma told him we used the straight kind. He had laughed and said he'd be sure to come. I guess he was just joking about the taste of chicory.

But we went to the church that night and leaders told us he was in very bad condition and had been taken to Birmingham [University Hospital]. Later we were told the ambulance had broken down a few miles outside of Selma, and another one was called and they wouldn't get him to the hospital until very late in the night.

It was that next day [Wednesday, March 10] that the mayor, Joe Smitherman, came down with the police, and they threw up a rope across the street and said we couldn't cross it, that all marches were banned.

It just seemed to make the people more determined; there were hundreds of us pressed up against it. We were on the one side and the troopers and police were on the other. We stood there all day, taking turns, and I don't think the singing ever stopped. I remember we kept getting reports all through the day about James Reeb, saying that he was in critical condition, lying there unconscious, dying—I think we all knew he was dying.

On March 11, Thursday, U.S. District Judge Frank M. Johnson, Jr., began the hearing in Montgomery on the petition by the SCLC to enjoin Governor Wallace, Sheriff Clark, and the state troopers from interfering with another planned march from Selma to Montgomery.

Nuns and ministers join Selma blacks who line up along a police barricade that came to be known as the Selma Wall. [Selma Police Photo]

Sheyann, center right, and Rachel, far right, wait their turn at a prayer vigil in front of Brown Chapel in 1965. [courtesy of *The Birmingham News*]

What I remember so clearly that day was the rain and this group of Catholic nuns going up to that rope—we now called it the Selma Wall—and kneeling down in front of the troopers and praying. I think that got to some of them, shamed them. They kept standing there, smoking cigarettes and looking nervous. I think when we began singing *We Shall Overcome* that some of them actually had tears in their eyes. It might have been from the cigarette smoke, but I don't think so. I believe we were getting to them. Me and Rachel and some other kids were up there by the nuns. We could have walked around the rope if we had wanted, but it was symbolic. We had to go through it, test what it stood for. Somebody made up the song called *Selma Wall* and we kept singing it, too.

> *We're gonna stay here 'til it falls,*
> *'Til it falls, 'til it falls,*
> *We're gonna stay here 'til it falls,*
> *In Selma, Alabama.*

Then the words said, "Hate is the word that built that wall," and the last stanza was, "Love is the word that'll make it fall,/in Selma, Alabama."

I remember there was a priest there talking with me and Rachel that day, and he was very distressed about the Reverend Reeb being attacked like that and being near death. And he was saying that—it was from the Bible—our lives are like flowers that are cut down. And he had picked this one little yellow flower as he talked, like it represented the Reverend Reeb's life.

And we took that flower and passed it from one to another as we knelt there in front of that rope.

In my own mind I was holding some hope that he would live. After being out in the rain most of the day, I had come into the house to get dry clothes and eat something. My momma had fixed me a plate, and after eating I had gone up to my room to change. That's when I noticed the singing from the street had stopped. And I heard Momma going out the door, so I hurried and threw something on and ran out after her. When I got out on the street I heard some of the women crying and everyone was kneeling down and nobody was saying anything. It was so quiet then, nobody had to tell me James Reeb had died.

The announcement had been made quietly by Selma's public-safety director, Wilson Baker. He had come up to the rope and said, "Reverend Reeb died earlier tonight. He never regained consciousness. I'm sorry."

I knelt down beside Rachel and we prayed to ourselves for awhile. I didn't cry. I just kept thinking how even though he had been white, he had been one of us, too. I kept thinking that he had come to help us, just because he was a good man who couldn't stand by and watch injustice continue. And I kept thinking that if he had stayed at our house for coffee that day, he would not have been on the street in the downtown when the white men came out of that Silver Moon Café looking for "white niggers." I kept thinking that over and over. If only he had stayed.

And Rachel, kneeling there with her head covered
with her coat parka, turned to me and I saw she had a
puzzled look on her face. And she had tears in her
eyes and she is shaking her head and she says to me,
"Why they have to do that, Shey? Why they have to
hit him like that?"
I didn't know.

CHAPTER TWENTY

"There must be in cases like this one . . . a 'constitutional bound-
ary line.' . . . it seems basic to our . . . principles that the extent of
the right to assemble, demonstrate and march peaceably along
the highways and streets in an orderly manner should be com-
mensurate with the enormity of the wrongs that are being pro-
tested and petitioned against.
"In this case, the wrongs are enormous.
"It is recognized that the plan as proposed [to march from
Selma to Montgomery] . . . reaches to the outer limits of what is
constitutionally allowed. However, the wrongs and injustices in-
flicted upon [blacks in Selma] have clearly exceeded—and continue to exceed—the outer limits of what is constitutionally
permissible."—United States District Judge Frank M. Johnson, Jr.,
March 17, 1965, in his order granting blacks the right to march
from Selma to Montgomery.

Rachel

When James Reeb died it tore away a little more of the
courage I'd found in the movement. It made me worry
again about who might be next. It made me worry,

would *I* be the one the next time. We were a defense-less people; we were women and we were children. And there was nothing at all we could do against clubs or guns, or tear gas and horses.

I think when I cried that night that he died I was also crying because I just knew there would be more of this. There would be more candles burning, more people praying in the rain, more flowers passed from hand to hand.

I not only was kneeling there, but I had my head laid down almost on the pavement while we prayed, and I was praying there would be a way to stop all of this, praying that maybe we could just pick up the telephone and call George Wallace and tell him that there had been enough suffering, that it was time to just let us come on over across the bridge and come to Montgomery, come on over and be free. All he would have to do to stop this was to listen to us and agree that, yes, we were right and should be free like the rest of the people. He could have done it and James Reeb and Jimmie Lee Jackson wouldn't have died. He could have done it.

Me and Sheyann used to walk about the church there and look for some sign that would tell us the Lord was on our side, that He was watching us. We'd look and we'd see a leaf falling, and we'd say that was the sign. And we'd know we were winning.

We'd see the moon shining down some nights and we'd say that was the sign. And we'd say we were winning.

We'd hear the wind blowing or hear the thunder. That was the sign, we'd say. We were winning.

So this night, very late, the night James Reeb died, we were out there with all these sad people, and so many of them were still crying. So we walked about the crowd, looking for a sign, because we needed that assurance. And we'd heard somebody—one of the ministers or nuns—say that when a good person dies the Lord hangs out a new star in the night. So we looked up for a shiny new star which would be the sign.

So we looked and looked, but the sky was full of clouds.

And I said to Sheyann, "There ain't no sign tonight."

And she says, "Keep lookin', Rachel, 'til we see it."

So we kept standing there, with our heads turned upward like that. And all of a sudden it started raining again, right in our faces.

And I yelled, "Shey, there ain't gonna be no sign."

But she's still looking up like that and all of a sudden she says, "The rain's the sign. The rain is."

And I looked up again, letting it just splatter all over my face and in my eyes. The sudden way it had started made me agree that it surely must be the sign. So we sat on the steps of Brown Chapel the whole night with a quilt over us, shivering and praying there. And we were convinced that this rain meant that even the Lord in Heaven was sad by James Reeb's death and He was joining us in our sadness, in our weeping.

But the most frightening thing that happened took place one afternoon when the rain had ended and the clouds in the sky began to break up and thin. We had been out there in the street singing. After several hours we had stopped to rest, and we were just standing around, talking and eating some sandwiches that someone had brought.

I'm not sure what it was that happened, then. But all of a sudden I heard someone shout something like, "Look at that! The sun! It's spinning around!" And I looked up and the sun had come out from behind the clouds—well, I mean, the clouds had thinned and you could see the sun and it was sort of bluish, hazylike. And as I looked it seemed like it was spinning about, whirling or something. I remember my stomach and chest seemed to go cold—it just made you stop and catch your breath.

And somebody yells, "It's going to fall!" And we all just fell on our knees, and people were shouting that the Lord was mad about things in Selma and now He was going to do something. We just knelt down in the water and started praying. But I kept looking up at that sun. It was like whorls of clouds were being spun about it—well, I don't really know what made it do that. But it did seem to be spinning about and going up and down. I had never seen anything like that before. There was a whole group of us there and we were scared, afraid the end of the world might be starting. I remember people were crying out, "Lord, save us! Lord, save us!" over and over like that. Well, it stopped then, that spinning motion, but we kept kneeling there for some time after that, praying. Later, I figured that that had to be the strongest sign the Lord had sent to us. But it was scary.

To this day I wonder about it. I'd heard of something like that happening once at Fatima when a girl had said she saw the Blessed Virgin Mary. But, anyway, it happened here in Selma—but I don't know for sure what it was.

During that time it seemed each day and each night was like the one before it; nothing changed. The rope stayed there, we stayed there, the troopers stayed there; we'd sing hour after hour until our throats became hoarse. The rain fell, fell almost constantly. The sun would come out briefly, then it would start raining again. We'd be soaked to the skin. It would turn warm; it would turn cold.

Signs. Signs that we were right. Day after day. For a whole week it went on.

On Monday, the fifteenth, everyone took a break and went inside to a television set. President Johnson was to deliver a speech about Selma and the right to vote.

I remember lying on the living room floor in front of the set, watching, listening. It seemed he was speaking directly to me.

"The effort of American Negroes to secure for themselves the full blessing of American life must be our cause, too. Because it is not just Negroes, but really, it is all of us who must overcome the crippling legacy of bigotry and injustice.

"And we shall overcome."

When he said that all the people in the room, my sisters, my parents, the ministers, all cried out and applauded. I just lay there watching, listening. Somebody *had* heard us.

And the president went on: "The real hero of the struggle is the American Negro. The cries of pain and the hymns and protests of oppressed people have summoned into convocation all the majesty of this great government."

Except for that one time, we just listened quietly. Once in a while I'd hear my mother or father agree with him a, "Um-hmm," but that was all. I remember after his speech going over to Sheyann's, and she was just sitting there in the living room, thinking about it.

And I said, "You hear that speech?"

And she says, "I heard it." Then after a long time she said, "But he's there in Washington, and we be down here by ourselves."

One day that week Wilson Baker, Selma's public-safety director, walked up to the rope, took a pair of shears, and cut it. I was there but didn't hear what he said. Later somebody told me he said, "I'm tired of hearing them sing about the damned thing."

It was another sign. We were winning.

Then, on March seventeenth, people began running through the crowd out in the street. And we all go running over there to see what it is and they tell us that the judge in Montgomery [Frank M. Johnson, Jr.] had ruled in our favor, and we're going to march to Montgomery, and the troopers and the sheriff's possemen can't stop us anymore.

We're marching, they tell us, over that river to the freedom land!

And I saw Shey and she was running toward me and we just grabbed each other and started hopping around. Everyone was shaking hands and hugging; some were shouting. I saw one woman crying, she was so happy. And as me and Shey jumped around it must have struck us both that this struggle was finally over. The struggle was over and we were going to be free at last. And folks were saying:

"Ain't nobody gonna turn us 'round."

"Ain't no horses gonna turn us 'round. And no troopers. No tear gas. No sheriff."

Nobody was gonna turn us 'round no more. *Nobody!*

CHAPTER.TWENTY-ONE

Judge Frank M. Johnson, Jr.'s order permitting the Selma-to-Montgomery march set off a frantic chain of events not only in Selma but, indeed, across the nation. Hundreds of people—the famous and the nameless—hurried to Selma to take part in the historic fifty-mile walk across part of the Alabama Black Belt. In Washington, President Lyndon Johnson ordered the Alabama

National Guard federalized to provide protection; he also ordered paratroopers to be prepared to join in the march, should trouble occur. In Selma, preparations were being made to ensure the availability of adequate food supplies, tenting and bedding, portable sanitary facilities, and campsites. By Saturday morning, March 20, the George Washington Carver Homes were awash with people. The march was to begin the following day, just two weeks after the rout at the bridge.

Sheyann

Our house was full of people. They'd sleep in sleeping bags on the living-room floor, in the upstairs hallway, anywhere there was space. It was that way everywhere. You had to stand in line to get into the bathroom.

What I remember most about those days just before the march was the large groups of people always out by the church singing freedom songs. They'd go on all through the night. I'd fall asleep listening to them.

Nothing like this had ever happened before in America; people from all over had come to join us because we were successful in dramatizing that there were wrongs in the South and the time had come to change them. It was more than the right to vote; it was also the way we had been treated.

Until Dr. King came to Selma, we had been too afraid even to ask if we could be free; folks were too timid to ask to vote.

But Judge Frank Johnson's order was going to change that. Not since Abraham Lincoln had a white man done so much to help us. And President Johnson was helping.

So as we gathered at the church on that Sunday [March 21], it was more than just a march to dramatize our desire to vote. It meant that we would get out in the sunshine and let everyone know that we were Americans, too; and that we were southerners, too; and that we were Alabamians and citizens of Selma, too.

So all this was coming about—this right to be free from fear—in Selma and it was coming about because of the courage of poor, ordinary black people who knew the time was here.

I remember on that Sunday that there were thousands of people gathered around the church. But from all those people I remember they got me and Rachel and we sang a song while some people recorded it for a record company [Folkways]. And later, before we started, a photographer took a picture of me and Rachel sitting on Dr. King's lap.

What I remember so much about that day was the happiness of the people. I had never seen them like that before. When we finished singing *We Shall Overcome*, we started off and went to the bridge and there were soldiers with rifles and bayonets everywhere, protecting us. Well, when we crossed that bridge and started on down the road for Montgomery, the people just seemed like something had been lifted from their shoulders. They were so proud, but it was a pride that was dignified. We had always maintained that dignity.

It was such a beautiful, sunshiny day. And I walked along with Rachel for awhile and we kept looking up at the sky. And there was a sign that somebody was carrying—a placard or banner, I mean—which said the whole thing that was on my mind.

It said that we weren't marching fifty miles; instead, we were marching to cover three hundred years.

My family and Rachel's family were all with us that day and we went about ten miles down the road. We were singing *Ain't Gonna Let Nobody Turn Me 'Round* as we came up to some buses pulled off alongside the road. We stopped there, and that's when Dr. King saw us.

"Are you marching all the way?" he asked, and the way he said it and the way he was smiling told me he was quite proud.

And I told him, "I don't know 'cause my momma said I had to come back home. She didn't give me permission."

"Aren't you tired?" he says.

And me and Rachel shrugged and grinned, and I said, "My feets and legs be tired, but my soul still feels like marchin'."

So he said that we had walked far enough for little girls and he wanted us to get on the bus and go back to Selma. So we said we'd do that and he touched us on the head and went on down the road.

I remember standing there a long time and watching those people marching along. I would never forget that sight.

And I said to Rachel, "It seem like we marchin' to Heaven today."

And she says, "Ain't we?"

We all drove over to Montgomery that following Thursday for the big rally in front of the Alabama Capitol. We had parked on the edge of the city and joined in the march for the last few miles, and it was just an endless stream of people moving through a light rain. I remember the huge throng of people—some said there were twenty-five thousand, some said as many as fifty thousand—just massed there in front, and Dr. King speaking to us, telling us that we had been on a long journey for freedom. He ended with the words, "Glory, glory, hallelujah," and repeated it several times, and each time everyone would cheer and it ended with a deafening roar.

As I look back on it, I think the real victory wasn't the fact that we went to Montgomery and had that rally. The real victory was just winning the *right* to do that. That fifty-mile march was symbolic. The real triumph had been on March the seventh at the bridge and at the church afterwards, when we turned a brutal beating into a nonviolent victory.   .

On that day of the rally in Montgomery, we had stayed for part of the entertainment in which some singers such as Peter, Paul, and Mary and Harry Belafonte had performed; but it was raining so hard that we finally drove back home.

It was later that night that we went to the church [Brown Chapel] and someone came in with the news that a woman had been shot to death in Lowndes County.

Viola Gregg Liuzzo, thirty-eight, of Detroit, Michigan, had transported a car full of marchers back to Selma that night and, accompanied by a young black man, Leroy Moton, was making the return trip to Montgomery. A car carrying armed Klansmen had followed her, pursuing at speeds up to eighty miles per hour. Overtaking her in Lowndes County, they had sped around and fired several shots into her car; one bullet struck her in the head, killing her almost instantly. Leroy Moton survived the attack and managed to bring the car to a halt alongside Highway 80.

Sheyann

I didn't know Mrs. Liuzzo; she was one of the hundreds of people who had come to Selma for the big march. I remember when they told us the news that night, everyone seemed sort of shocked. We were all tired and drained of emotion. We had just made this monumental march to Montgomery, this pilgrimage to seek the right to be fully free, and we felt we had finally won it. The killing would not stop that. But it did make us realize that death and violence might still be a part of our lives and [that] the resistance might not stop. The bullets that had been fired at her car could have been aimed at any of the hundreds of cars making the trip that night. It had been a senseless crime, a cowardly action. The church was quiet. All we could do was shake our heads.

I think it was the next day that there was a memorial service for this woman who had come to help us. It was also reported that day that four Ku Klux Klansmen had been arrested for the murder. And we also learned that they had been in Selma that night, driving right by Brown Chapel, looking for blacks to attack. It was frightening, because Rachel and I had been outside the church. Only the presence of armed troops probably kept them from attacking some of us.

In the years that followed, we could never go to Montgomery without pointing out milestones along the way: Here was the spot where I had marched to that first day and then boarded a bus to return home, the place where Dr. King talked with us.

Or there was the place, in a meadow, where the marchers camped the second night. Or there was the place we had driven to on the third day, when it was raining, and watched those who walked the entire distance (I didn't, because my momma said it was too far) and saw them resting under some trees that were covered in long wisps of Spanish Moss.

And finally, there was the place where the woman from Detroit had been ambushed and shot to death.

The land looks much the same. I hope someday there might be some markers put down for people who come to visit, so they might have at least some idea of what happened here.

CHAPTER TWENTY-TWO

On August 6, 1965, the voting-rights bill that President Johnson had sent to Congress in March—after the incident at the Pettus Bridge in Selma—was signed into law. Its birth and enactment was credited to the efforts of hundreds of anonymous black men, women, and children in Selma. "Today, the Negro story and the American story fuse and blend," said the president, speaking at the Capitol Rotunda in front of the Lincoln Memorial. "Let me now say to every Negro in this country: You must register. You must vote. You must learn, so your choice advances your interest and the interest of our beloved nation."

Just fourteen days later, a young Episcopalian seminary student, Jonathan Daniels, 26, of Keene, New Hampshire, was shot and killed in Hayneville, Alabama, the seat of Lowndes County, twenty-five miles from Selma. Wounded in the attack was a Catholic priest, Richard F. Morrisroe of Chicago. Both had lived with Rachel West's family in Selma. They had been in Lowndes County to help with voter registration and had been arrested on August 14 for taking part in a demonstration. The shooting occurred just minutes after the two men had been released on bond.

Rachel

It's hard to say that you have won something when it means you lose a friend like Jonathan Daniels. He had come to live with me and my family back in February of 1965.

He stayed with us through the marches, then left us for awhile to return to New Hampshire. But later he came back to help with getting the people out to the registrars' offices. He said that there were people who were still afraid—especially in the rural areas outside of Selma—to go to the courthouses.

He wanted to help them overcome that fear.

What I remember about him is that he was like a boy; he was youthful, always smiling. His eyes were clear and steady. He was friendly. He was, most of all, very gentle.

He was a part of our family. He was a part of Sheyann's family, too. In a way, he was a member of every black family in Selma, in those days.

I know there were times when he must have been frightened, but he never showed it.

There was the day when he went to the post office to mail a letter to his family. And while there, he told us later, several white men came up to him and one of them asked him:

"Are you that white nigger?"

And he didn't answer them.

So they asked him again: "You that white nigger?"

Jonathan had walked away then. Surely it had frightened him, but as he told us about it, he smiled sadly, like he might have felt sorry for the men. And my mother told him she was sorry he had to put up with such things.

"It's all right," he had said. "When they asked me if I was the white nigger, I didn't answer out loud, Mrs. West. But in my heart something inside me cried out, 'Yes!' And I am."

I remember one day after many of our people had been arrested and there was talk of more trouble before us, I was standing outside in the apartment yard watching some of the other children play. Jonathan saw me and came and knelt down beside me.

"Why aren't you playing with the others?" he asks. And I had shrugged. "I don't know why."

So he stares at me very seriously and puts an arm around me. "You afraid of something?"

And I told him I was thinking about the sheriff's posse and some of the bad things that had been happening.

"You don't have to be afraid any more," he said. "I'll watch you and make sure nothing or nobody bothers you. All right?"

But I didn't know. So all of a sudden he picked me up and tossed me up in the air, spinning around and around. "Now are you afraid?" he asked. And I started laughing then. He kept spinning around and throwing me up and catching me. Finally I yelled that I wasn't afraid, and he put me down.

He was always playing with us children.

Jonathan went away for a while during the early spring—it was after the Selma-to-Montgomery march —but he promised he would come back. He called us often on the telephone, and we'd all talk to him.

Finally, he did come back, and my father and mother went to Montgomery to pick him up at the airport. When they pulled up in the car and I saw him, I tore across the yard to him and he picked me up. I remember I was squealing with joy to see him, and kissed him on the cheek.

He continued to live with us even though he began leaving each day with some of the other civil-rights workers to go to Lowndes County to help with the registration efforts there. One day he didn't come back and I was told he had been arrested and put in jail.

I was outside playing that day in August when my mother called me, and I saw she was crying. I asked her what was the matter.

"Our friend is dead," she said. Just like that. Then she hugged me close. "Our friend is dead, Rachel."

"Who?" I asked. But I knew. "Jonathan? They killed Jonathan?"

"Yes, they did," she said. "They killed Jonathan."

I didn't want to believe it. Who could kill or even hurt someone as kind as him? But my mother said she had received a telephone call, and it was true.

I must have cried the whole night long. Of all the things that had happened during that movement, nothing touched me as deeply as his death. I remember I had gone to Sheyann's house then and we stood out in the yard; there were other children there. Some of them were crying, too. I remember I kept looking across the yard and thinking I'd see him running toward us, laughing or smiling as he always did.

He had been shot down by a man in front of a store. He had died the way he had lived, smiling and reaching out to shake the man's hand, trying to be a friend. He had died trying to make peace. I'm sure that if he had had a choice about it, he'd have preferred to have lived awhile; he was a very young person. But I also think that he preferred to die for a cause.

My mother went to New Hampshire for his funeral, I remember. Some people had sent the money for her plane ticket up there. Jonathan's family wanted her to be there, so my mother went to represent the Negro people of Selma, the ones he had died for.

In later years, a day-care center was built in Selma and named after Jonathan. My mother worked there. She still does at this time.

She could have found work at other places, but she wanted to be there. I can understand why.

CHAPTER TWENTY-THREE

February 9, 1979. Sheyann Webb is a senior at Tuskegee Institute, where she has been a member of the choir and coordinator of the Student Government Association. She is a beautiful young woman who placed second in a beauty pageant, winning the bathing suit competition. Earlier, at Selma High School, she was an honor-roll student and a cheerleader.

Sheyann

When I turned eighteen back in 1974, the first thing I did was go down to the courthouse and register to vote. That was a promise I'd made myself when I was a kid. But you'd be surprised how many people haven't done it. After all we went through back in 1965. I worked on a voter registration drive in 1974 in Lowndes County. They still live on the land that used to be plantations. It made me sick. They told me they didn't have any use in registering. I couldn't believe it. Dr. King had put his life on the line for them and they tell me that. It seemed like he died for nothing, in some cases.

In 1975, in March, we had a commemoration rally and march to observe the tenth anniversary of Bloody Sunday. Mrs. [Coretta] King came here and we had a church full of people at Brown Chapel. Boy, did that bring back memories! It was lightning and thundering that night, but the people came out. And there were troopers there, but they were there to protect us, I guess. And the next day, a Saturday, we marched out over the bridge again, and I could see those horsemen again—in my mind, I mean. But it was like old times that day. I got up there and led them singing *Ain't Gonna Let Nobody Turn me 'Round.* I only wished Dr. King could have been here for that. He'd have been so proud.

I remember when he was here the last time before he was murdered—I think it must have been a month or two before. And we had a big turnout for him. He talked with me, and we talked about visiting with his family in Atlanta. And he had told me about the poor-peoples' march to Washington he was planning. And when he left he had kissed me goodbye. I didn't know it would be the last time.

When I heard the news that night—it was a bulletin on television—I went up to my room and cried. And later that night—I don't think I slept at all—I sat on the bed and took my pencil and notebook and wrote a little essay about "My Pal, Dr. King." I was twelve when he was killed. I had always thought when I grew up that I'd go with him and work for civil rights and the dream he'd had for making life better for poor folks. So when he was killed, I made up my mind that I'd join that march to Washington—because it was his

Sheyann Webb, at age 19, with Mrs. Coretta King on a Selma visit.

march. I was in the sixth grade then. So one day I saw all these people with that mule pulling a wagon out in front of them, and there was old Hosea [Williams] leading them, coming through Selma. I just dropped everything then and went with them.

I just felt it was more important than school. My parents didn't know it. I missed so much school that year that I was flunked and had to repeat. But, anyway, my mother and dad finally caught up with me later in Montgomery and made me come home.

One day in 1975, they called me up to the mayor's office to have a picture made with Mr. Smitherman and Wilson Baker and Reverend Reese; it had to do with the tenth anniversary. And Mr. Baker looks at me and says he remembers me running down off the bridge that day. And he apologizes for what had happened.

I think of those days all the time. I can't explain how I feel about the church—Brown Chapel. It's like a shrine to us. We'd be there day and night, singing and praying together.

I remember waking up some mornings and it seemed death was all around us. Sometimes I couldn't eat. But I'd go to the church and things would be better then. I mean, I'd be scared, but I'd be ready. I knew that if I had to die, well, I wanted to die for what we believed in. I really did believe in it. Sometimes, I think if I hadn't been so young, I might not have been so active. Because as a child, those songs meant so much to me and to Rachel. They held the movement together at times. And we'd stay together. I don't think anybody in this country has ever lived in such a time. There was such a togetherness.

I don't know what I'll do for sure when I graduate from Tuskegee. Maybe I'll return to Selma and run for mayor, I don't know.

People are always asking me what I remember about 1965. I guess the thing that stands out about Bloody Sunday was those horsemen. I still dream about them, even now, coming through the tear gas. And the riders were wearing those masks. And swinging their clubs at everybody. It was really awful. I still don't understand why they had to do it—why they had to be so hateful.

Maybe it was because they didn't understand. Maybe they were more afraid of us than we were of them, I don't know.

But now I think of all the good things that happened. We were so close, all of us. And Dr. King used to talk about a beloved community, a place where black and white could live in love and understanding.

When we had the anniversary march in 1975 I had the feeling—as I walked across that bridge with Rachel and the others—that maybe we were near that dream. I still hope we are. A beloved community. I hope we find it here. Because Selma is my home, too, just as it is for a lot of white folks.

In those days we had a cause, something to strive for. Today, people don't seem to have anything to

Sheyann Webb, at age 19, on the Edmund Pettus Bridge during the tenth anniversary observance of Bloody Sunday.

keep them going. They just go around trying to make a living. But we had our freedom to gain. And it was such a beautiful thing. I remember once—after the beating at the bridge—there were so many people at Brown Chapel that Reverend Reese told me to take the children down to First Baptist, which is about two blocks down the street, and we went and marched up a storm. I'd yell, "What do you want?" And they'd yell, "Freedom!" It was like that.

I could never understand the hatred some of the whites showed toward us. I was just a kid and they'd yell at me. Yet, we all prayed to the same God. I couldn't understand the hatred. I couldn't understand the segregation.

What happened here in 1965 is history now. I know that. We have to go on. But I can never forget it. I never will. If I live to be a hundred-and-three, I'll still have my own little commemoration on March the seventh. I think of it often—not just that day, but all the days of the movement here in Selma. I'm just so happy that I could be a part of a thing that touched our souls. I am so proud of the people who did something in 1965 that was truly amazing. We were just people, ordinary people, and we did it.

CHAPTER TWENTY-FOUR

Rachel West Nelson, twenty-three, married, the mother of two children, works in Selma as an operator with the South Central Bell telephone company. She is a beautiful woman, tall and slim, whose eyes still have a childlike, somewhat mischievous sparkle to them. It is March 1979. She stands near Brown Chapel AME Church.

Rachel

It may sound silly to some, but I can come out here and it seems I can still hear all the singing that went on back in those times in 1965. We spent a lot of time here, Shey and me. A lot of us did. We were here to get our freedom. I know we'd stay out here and it would be raining and it would be cold, but we'd stay all through the nights. Yes, sir.

What happened right here will never be forgotten. I remember me and Shey being here and Dr. King talking to us and asking us about freedom. Because that's what it was about in those days. Freedom. Wasn't nobody giving us nothing unless we went out and fought for it, fought for it nonviolently. And I was scared some of the time—a lot of the time, to tell the truth. Because we didn't know what might happen. People were always talking about snipers coming by, that sort of thing. And being a kid, you believed it. So it took everything you had inside you to come out here. But the people would sing with us, and we'd help each other overcome the fear.

We really didn't have much in those days. I mean there wasn't much food, and the clothes I had didn't even fit me very well. The movement is all we black folks had.

Rachel West Nelson in 1979 in front of historic Brown Chapel AME Church, rallying point of the 1965 voting-rights demonstrations.

But it was such a beautiful thing. It drew people together. Shey was a Baptist, I was a Catholic. But no matter what we were, we all went to the meetings and the rallies at the church, Brown Chapel AME Church. And Catholic priests and nuns were there, too, because the movement was above what faith you were. It was a thing that was of the people. And it was of the Lord, no matter what church you belonged to. We put a lot of faith in Dr. King, a lot of faith in ourselves in those days. But we knew our deepest trust had to be in the Lord, because what we were doing was in the Lord's hand. We really believed that, Shey and me.

[A pause. Then she laughs.]

I was carrying my first baby when they announced there was going to be a commemoration march in 1975. And my husband and my family tell me, "You shouldn't be out there marching. You need to rest." But, shoot, I couldn't rest that day. Not me. If that baby had been due that very day, I'd have been out there marching. I couldn't miss it. It tired me out going out across the bridge, but I wouldn't have it any other way. When me and Shey were kids, we had talked about things like this when we grew up—having babies and all. We knew what we were doing in 1965 wasn't just for us, but for the children still to be born. We wanted them born free. So the babies I've had have been born into a free society. They can grow up to be full citizens. It means a lot to me to be able to say that.

But you can't think about those times without being

sad, thinking about Jonathan Daniels and Dr. King. I don't think a day goes by that I don't think about them. I was really close to Jonathan. There was nobody like him, not like Jonathan. I've been over there to Lowndes County to see where he died.

When I think of Dr. King, well, there's so much to remember. Like the time he came to Selma in 1968, not long before he was killed. My mother and my sisters and me went to see him at the church. And when he came in, all the people started singing *Battle Hymn of the Republic*. "Glory, glory, hallelujah." Did we ever sing it that night. And we all stood up as we sang, and Dr. King just beamed at us, he was so happy and proud.

So later, when I heard that he'd been shot and killed in Memphis, I just cried and cried. I really felt so alone then. First Jonathan, I thought, and now Dr. King. And I went off by myself and thought about him, how he'd kissed me hello and goodbye so often. And I thought about us singing that song and it seemed like a message or something, those words, you know, "His truth is marching on."

And that night I could see him smiling at me, the way he had when he'd ask Shey and me what we wanted. And it dawned on me that he was such a great man and I had had the opportunity to know him. I cried for him that night, but I knew all the things he stood for would not die—things like justice, equality, compassion, love, working to make life a little better for poor people, all those things.

Even today, just as I can hear the singing on this street, so can I sometimes almost see Dr. King out here again. Even today, his truth is marching on. Yes, sir.

He taught us to be the best of whatever we were. We couldn't all be Dr. Kings here. We couldn't all be leaders. But he inspired so many of us to get out and do what we could to help ourselves be free. In our case, that meant getting out to win the right to vote.

To vote, you have to be free. Slaves can't vote. Only free people.

What happened in Selma was more than getting the right to vote. We first had to set ourselves free. After three hundred years, we had to set ourselves free. That's what Dr. King was telling us, when he said we couldn't stay on the sidelines, that we had to get out and march.

In Selma, getting the right to vote didn't set us free.

No sir. In Selma, we got the right to vote because we had *set* ourselves free.

AFTERWORD

These interviews with Sheyann Webb and Rachel West Nelson ended in March 1979. They were concluded in a Selma quite different from the Selma of early 1965. Certainly Sheyann and Rachel were much changed. Sheyann was preparing for a spring 1979 graduation at Tuskegee Institute. Rachel was working as a telephone operator and was married.

But much remained the same in Selma. Brown Chapel AME Church still dominated the street where the marches commenced, but the name had been changed from Sylvan Street to Martin Luther King Jr. Boulevard. The Webbs and the Wests still lived next door to each other in the George Washington Carver Homes. Clark School, though part of the city's integrated system, remained largely black. The Edmund Pettus Bridge, with its hump of silver girding, still stood, looming over the city's downtown area. Joseph T. Smitherman was still the mayor, but he planned to retire in July; and he had, in his own words, "matured since 1965." Four of the ten members of the city council were black.

The last interview was held on a mellow, springlike afternoon. Rachel had the day off and came to her mother's apartment with her two children, Chad, four, and Cicely, not quite two. I had talked to Sheyann a few days earlier.

Rachel brought an old copy of a *Selma Times-Journal* and showed me a somewhat tattered page. "See this?" she asked, pointing. It was the voter list published for an earlier election, before her marriage. The names Krisandra Sheyann Webb and Rachel West were printed there, close to each other.

"We're on there," she said. "If 1965 hadn't happened the way it did in Selma, you wouldn't see them there."

A pause. Then: "You know, in those times, you know what we had to eat most of the time? Rice. Rice all the time. Rice and coffee. I lived on that. Didn't have much milk, so we 'd drink it [the coffee] black." She laughs. "Maybe that's why we could stay up late and be out at the church all them nights."

Outside, the sun sparkled on the faded red brick of the apartments. She held a hand above her eyes and stared at them.

"It seems like ages ago," she said. "And sometimes it seems like it was just yesterday. I know it'll never go away."

She stood and watched, a quiet smile lighting her face, as a dozen children romped about playing kickball in the yard where she and Sheyann Webb had been terrorized by Sheriff Jim Clark's mounted posse on the seventh day of March, 1965.

I HAD A DREAM
THEY GAVE THEIR LIVES
to overcome injustice and secure the right to vote for all Americans
JAMES J. REEB
Boston
VIOLA GREGG LIUZZO
Detroit
JIMMY LEE JACKSON
Marion, Alabama
DEDICATED
DR. MARTIN L. KING JR.

1/0